BARRON'S

EARLY ACHIEVER

GRADE 4

ENGLISH LANGUAGE ARTS WORKBOOK

ACTIVITIES & PRACTICE

REVIEW · UNDERSTAND · DISCOVER

Published by Kaplan North America, LLC, d/b/a Barron's Educational Series
1515 West Cypress Creek Road
Fort Lauderdale, Florida 33309
www.barronseduc.com

ISBN 978-1-5062-8157-5

10 9 8 7 6 5 4 3 2 1

Kaplan North America, LLC, d/b/a Barron's Educational Series print books are available at special quantity discounts to use for sales promotions, employee premiums, or educational purposes. For more information or to purchase books, please call the Simon & Schuster special sales department at 866-506-1949.

Photo Credits: Page 2 ©Monkey Business Images/Shutterstock, Page 3 ©jannoon /Shutterstock, Page 7 ©Stefano Tinti/Shutterstock, Page 10 ©Sebastian Kaulitzki/Shutterstock, Page 14 ©Volt Collection/Shutterstock, Page 15 ©Everett Historica/Shutterstock, Page 16 ©HUANG Zheng/Shutterstock, Page 22 ©360b/Shutterstock, Page 28 (background paintbrushes) ©Pinkyone/Shutterstock, (figures) ©Hein Nouwens/Shutterstock, Page 29 ©Everett Historical/Shutterstock, Page 41 ©catwalker/Shutterstock, Page 43© Ron Ellis/Shutterstock, Page 45 ©Incarnatus/ Shutterstock, Page 54 ©Blue Vista Design/Shutterstock, Page 48 ©Jurgen Ziewe/Shutterstock, Page 56 ©Adam Vilimek/Shutterstock, Page 60 ©Steve Byland/Shutterstock, Page 61 ©Monkey Business Images/Shutterstock, Page 66 ©altanaka/Shutterstock, Page 69 ©Erik Harrison/Shutterstock, Page 73 ©Bruce Rolff/Shutterstock, Page 75 ©ajman/Shutterstock, Page 77 ©FloridaStock/Shutterstock, Page 78 ©Kevin Le/Shutterstock, Page 83 ©Fish and Wildlife Service/Shutterstock, Page 84 ©Dennis W. Donohue/Shutterstock, Page 87 ©chrisdorney/Shutterstock, Page 89 ©Jianghaistudio/Shutterstock, Page 90 ©PanStock/Shutterstock, Page 92 ©sakhorn/Shutterstock, Page 97 ©Tory Kallman/Shutterstock, Page 102 ©Ron Ellis/Shutterstock, Page 103 ©Kipling/Shutterstock (portrait), ©Nicku/Shutterstock (typewriter), Page 105 ©Anton Lunkov/Shutterstock, Page 106 ©Dennis Jacobsen/Shutterstock, Page 112 ©IgorGolovniov /Shutterstock, Page 117 ©Danilo Sanino/Shutterstock, Page 124 ©Samuel Borges Photography/Shutterstock, Page 125 ©J. Palys/Shutterstock (jewels), Page 132 ©AAresTT/Shutterstock, Page 136 ©Zakharchenko Anna/Shutterstock, Page 138 ©Galushko Sergey/Shutterstock, Page 145 ©Osijan/Shutterstock, Page 150 ©Ron and Joe/Shutterstock, Page 153 ©Sean Locke Photography/Shutterstock (chest), ©Ralf Juergen Kraft/Shutterstock (Trojan horse), Page 155 ©Blue Ring Media/Shutterstock, Page 159© K. Jensen/Shutterstock, Page 165 ©natrot/Shutterstock, Page 166 ©natrot/Shutterstock

Introduction

Barron's Early Achiever workbooks are based on sound educational practices and include both parent-friendly and teacher-friendly explanations of specific learning goals and how students can achieve them through fun and interesting activities and practice. This exciting series mirrors the way English Language Arts is taught in the classroom. *Early Achiever Grade 4 English Language Arts* presents these skills through different units of related materials that reinforce each learning goal in a meaningful way. The Review, Understand, and Discover sections assist parents, teachers, and tutors in helping students apply skills at a higher level. Additionally, students will become familiar and comfortable with the manner of presentation and learning, as this is what they experience every day in the classroom. These factors will help early achievers master the skills and learning goals in English Language Arts and will also provide an opportunity for parents to play a larger role in their children's education.

Learning Goals for English Language Arts

The following explanation of educational goals is based on the skills that your child will learn in the fourth grade.

Reading Foundational Skills

Fluency

Your student will do/learn the following:

- Read on-level text with purpose and understanding
- Read on-level prose and poetry orally with accuracy, appropriate rate, and expression on successive readings
- Use context to confirm or self-correct word recognition and understanding, rereading as necessary

Reading Skills

Key Ideas and Details

Your student will do/learn the following:

- Refer to details and examples in a text to explain what the text says explicitly and when drawing inferences from the text
- Determine the main idea or theme of a text, story, drama, or poem from details in the text and summarize the text
- Describe a character, setting, or event in a story or drama by drawing on details in the text
- Explain events, procedures, ideas, or concepts in a historical, scientific, or technical text, including what happened and why, based on information in the text

Text Structure

Your student will do/learn the following:

- Determine the meaning of general academic and domain-specific words and phrases in a text relevant to a grade 4 topic or subject area
- Determine meanings of words and phrases used in a text, including those that allude to significant characters found in mythology
- Describe the overall structure (e.g., chronology, comparison, cause/effect, problem/solution) of events, ideas, concepts, or information in a text
- Explain major differences between poems, drama, and prose, and refer to the structural elements of poems (e.g., verse, rhythm, meter) and drama (e.g., casts of characters, settings, descriptions, dialogue, stage directions) when writing or speaking about a text
- Compare and contrast the point of view from which different stories are narrated, including the difference between first- and third-person narration
- Compare and contrast a firsthand and secondhand account of the same event or topic, describe the differences in focus and the information provided

Evaluate Text

Your student will do/learn the following:

- Interpret information presented visually, orally, or quantitatively (e.g., charts, graphs, diagrams, time lines, animations, or interactive elements on web pages) and explain how information contributes to the understanding of a text

- Make connections between a story or drama and a visual or oral presentation of the text, identifying where each version reflects specific descriptions and directions in the text

- Explain how an author uses reasons and evidence to support particular points in a text

- Compare and contrast the treatment of similar themes and topics (e.g., opposition of good and evil) and patterns of events (e.g., the quest) in stories, myths, and traditional literature from different cultures

- Integrate information from two texts on the same topic in order to write or speak about the subject knowledgeably

Writing Skills

Text Types and Purposes

Your student will do/learn the following:

- Write opinion pieces (which includes: introducing the topic clearly, stating an opinion, and creating an organizational structure in which related ideas are grouped; providing reasons supported by facts and details; linking opinions and reasons using words or phrases such as "for instance" and "in addition"; and providing a concluding statement related to the opinion presented)

- Write informative/explanatory texts (which includes: introducing a topic clearly and grouping related information in paragraphs and sections; using formatting such as headings, illustrations, and multimedia to aid comprehension; developing the topic with facts, definitions, concrete details, quotations, and examples; linking ideas with words or phrases such as "another," "for example," "also," and "because"; using precise language and domain-specific vocabulary to inform or explain; and providing a concluding statement or section related to the information presented)

- Write narratives (which includes: establishing a situation and introducing a narrator and/or characters; organizing an event sequence; using dialogue and description to develop experiences and events or show the response of characters to situations; using a variety of transitional words and phrases to manage the sequence of events; and providing a conclusion that follows from the narrated experiences or events)

Produce and Publish Writing

With the help of an adult or peer, your student will do/learn the following:

- Produce clear and coherent writing in which the development and organization are appropriate to task, purpose, and audience

- Develop and strengthen writing as needed by planning, revising, and editing

Learning Goals for English Language Arts

- Use technology, including the Internet, to produce and publish writing as well as interact and collaborate with others; demonstrate sufficient command of keyboarding skills to type a minimum of one page per single sitting

Research
Your student will do/learn the following:

- Conduct short research projects that build knowledge through investigation of different aspects of a topic
- Recall information from experiences or gather information from print and digital sources; take notes and categorize information; and provide a list of sources
- Draw evidence from literary or informational texts to support analysis, reflection, and research

Language Skills

Conventions of Standard English
Your student will do/learn the following:

- Use relative pronouns (who, whose, whom, which, that) and relative adverbs (where, when, why)
- Form and use progressive verb tenses (e.g., I was walking, I am walking, I will be walking)
- Use modal auxiliaries to convey various conditions (e.g., may, can, must)
- Order adjectives within sentences according to conventional patterns (e.g., a small, red bag rather than a red, small bag)
- Form and use prepositional phrases
- Produce complete sentences, recognizing and correcting inappropriate fragments and run-ons
- Correctly use frequently confused words (e.g., to, too, two; there, their, they're)
- Use correct capitalization
- Use commas and quotation marks to mark direct speech and quotations from a text
- Use a comma before a coordinating conjunction in a compound sentence
- Spell grade-appropriate words correctly, consulting references as needed

Knowledge of Language
Your student will do/learn the following:

- Choose words and phrases to convey ideas precisely
- Choose punctuation for effect
- Differentiate between contexts that call for formal English (e.g., presenting ideas) and situations where informal discourse is appropriate (e.g., small-group discussion)

Vocabulary
Your student will do/learn the following:

- Determine meanings of unknown and multiple-meaning words and phrases based on grade 4 reading and content using a range of strategies
- Use context (e.g., definitions, examples, or restatements in a text) as a clue to the meaning of a word or phrase
- Use common, grade-appropriate Greek and Latin affixes and roots as clues to the meaning of a word (e.g., telegraph, telephone, photograph, autograph)
- Consult reference material (e.g., dictionary, glossary, thesaurus), both in print and digital, to find the pronunciation and determine the meaning of key words or phrases
- Demonstrate understanding of figurative language, word relationships, and nuances in word meanings
- Explain the meaning of simple similes and metaphors in context
- Recognize and explain the meanings of common idioms, adages, and proverbs
- Demonstrate understanding of words by relating them to their opposites (antonyms) and to words with similar but not identical meanings (synonyms)

Contents

Contents

Reading Foundational Skills

Fluency: Read with Purpose and Understanding

In this first section, you will work with an adult to help you practice and/or learn the art of fluent reading. Fluency means reading with accuracy and speed and understanding what you read. You will learn to read aloud correctly with purpose, ease, and good expression. Reading properly with expression and with as few mistakes as possible is important for your reading progress. Why? Think about this. Fluency provides a connection between recognizing and understanding words. When reading quietly, fluent readers will group words together so that they recognize them right away. When reading aloud, there is a natural quality to their reading that is full of expression.

Whether you are a fluent reader already or are working toward this goal, keep practicing so that you continue to grow in your reading abilities.

Let's begin!

Adults:

Time your student reading aloud for one minute, and cross out any words that were eliminated or misread. At the end of one minute, mark the last word read and allow your student to finish reading the text. Count the total number of errors and subtract that from the number of words read. This will give you the total number of words read per minute.

TOTAL NUMBER OF WORDS – NUMBER OF ERRORS = WORDS READ PER MINUTE

Over an extended period of time, your student's fluency should increase by the number of words read per minute.

Unit 1 (September)	Unit 2 (December)	Unit 3 (March)	Unit 4 (June)
110	120	130	140

Getting a New Pet

Imagine being told that you are going to get a new pet. Exciting news, isn't it? What will	18
this pet be? A dog? A hamster? A cat? Getting a new pet can be a lot of fun. But caring for a	41
pet is a huge **responsibility**.	46
Before getting a pet, here are some things you should do to make sure your house	62
is ready.	64

- Look at your house and yard with an adult. Do you see anything that could hurt   80
  your pet? Holes in the yard and fence are dangerous if you have a dog. Even a   97
  swimming pool can be a danger for new pets.   106

- If your animal will stay indoors, check for loose wires. To a pet, they may look   122
  like toys.   124

Now that you know what to do to get your home ready, let's talk about the four basic	142
things all pets need—food, water, shelter, and love. Most animals need to be fed at least	159
once or twice a day. Be sure to ask your veterinarian or the pet store workers for the	177
right food and feeding information. When you feed your new pet, it should be in a quiet	194
and protected place. You want your pet to feel safe and comfortable. Just like you need	210
water, remember that your pet needs water, too. To be sure it is always fresh and clean,	227
the water in the bowl should be changed twice a day, or more if your pet drinks a lot!	246
Whether it's a tank, cage, or bed, your pet needs a place to call home. Outdoor pets need	264
to be protected from the cold, wind, sun, and rain. It is easy to think of pets as outside	283
pets, but bring your pet indoors at night, if possible. This will protect it from wild	299
animals, cars, and bad weather.	304
Finally, new pets need lots of love. This means giving them attention. Pets love attention	319
as much as you do. Giving hugs, kisses, scratches, and love will make your pet feel great.	336
Remember, a new pet is like a new member of your family. They need to feel welcomed and	354
wanted.	355

Words read in 1 minute – errors = WPM

CHECK FOR UNDERSTANDING

Adults: After your early achiever has finished reading, ask for a brief summary of the story so you can check comprehension. Write the summary on the lines below.

_____

_____

_____

GUIDED QUESTIONS

Use "Getting a New Pet" to answer the following questions.

1. According to the author, what should you look for around the house and in the yard before getting a new pet?

_____

_____

2. Reread this sentence.

   "But caring for a pet is a huge **responsibility**."

   Based on your understanding of the word **responsibility**, list two responsibilities that are mentioned in the text.

_____

_____

3. Why do you think new pets need love and affection?_____

_____

_____

4. Why are places to call home so important for pets? _____

_____

_____

Atlas, the Incredible Robot

Technology can be a powerful aid to people. Computers and even robots have been made to   16
help people with daily and sometimes difficult tasks. Whether it's cleaning the carpet floor or   31
saving reports to a hard drive, technology has played an important role in our world today.   47

The Need for Robotics   51

The Department of Defense (DoD), a branch of the federal government, is responsible for   65
helping people during disasters. However, some natural disasters, such as tornadoes and   77
earthquakes, pose many risks to human workers. The DoD wants to lower this risk.   91

DARPA Robotics Challenge (DRC)   95

How can the DoD help those in need while still keeping human workers safe? In 2013, the   112
DoD created a challenge for this very reason. In the DARPA Robotics Challenge (DRC),   126
teams must build ground robots. These ground robots are needed to help in serious   140
situations that could be challenging for people. For example, DARPA robots would be able   154
to use tools and vehicles in times of danger—situations that would otherwise put people at   170
risk. Each team must create a human-supervised robot that is able to complete tough tasks   186
in unsafe environments. The teams that develop the best robot compete in the DRC finals.   201
The team that wins the finals will have the privilege of the government using its robot for   218
years on into the future.   223

Meet Atlas, the Robot   227

One of the **front-runners** of the DRC competition is Atlas. Atlas is an amazing robot. At   244
a whopping 330 pounds, this six-foot-two machine will compete in the robotics challenge.   259
Imagine having to move a heavy tree in order to save a person's life. This could be very   277
difficult for one human alone. By contrast, Atlas is made to overcome such challenges. Like a   293
human being, it has joints that help it to be capable of many natural movements. However,   309
Atlas is much more powerful than the average person. It is designed to climb and work   325
through harsh environments. With two sets of hands and super strength, Atlas is considered   339
"advanced" technology because it is able to assist human beings in any disaster response.   353

Up for the Challenge   357

There are seven teams competing in the DARPA Robotics Challenge. Each team will have an   372
"Atlas" of its own to showcase. All of the Atlas robots cannot be winners, but one special   389
Atlas will be chosen to lead a new charge of super-powered robots. May the best robot win!   407

Words read in 1 minute − errors = WPM

CHECK FOR UNDERSTANDING

Adults: After your early achiever has finished reading, ask for a brief summary of the story so you can check comprehension. Write the summary on the lines below.

_____

_____

_____

GUIDED QUESTIONS

Use "Atlas, the Incredible Robot" to answer the following questions.

1. According to the author, why does the Department of Defense have a great need for robots?

    _____

    _____

2. Reread this sentence from the article.

    "One of the **front-runners** of the DRC competition is Atlas."

    Based on your understanding of the other words in the sentence, what is the meaning of the phrase **front-runners**?

    _____

    _____

3. How is Atlas similar to a human being? _____

    _____

    _____

4. How is Atlas different from a human being?

    _____

    _____

    _____

The Art of the Postal Stamp

Postal stamps are not only used to mail packages. In the United States, postal stamps are	16
also considered creative works of art. In 2003, the Smithsonian National Postal Museum	29
opened an exhibit, or public display, of over 100 original stamps that have been used for a	46
half-century.	48

How Postal Stamps are Created	53

Have an idea for a stamp? Many stamp designs have been suggested by people like you!	69
That's right. Any person can send a letter to the United States Post Office with an idea for	87
a stamp! After the letters have been received, the Citizens' Stamp Advisory Committee	100
(CSAC) meets four times each year to review these letters and select each stamp's subject.	115
The Postal Service Art Director then selects a style and theme for each stamp. This	130
person performs research, selects artists, and submits designs to the CSAC. The artist then	144
develops pencil sketches that turn into a beautiful final stamp design.	155
Developing a stamp is no easy process. It can take two years or more to create one! One	173
example is the design process for the Looney Tunes stamp series. In the first step, artists	189
from Warner Brothers, the company that makes the Looney Tunes, developed a lot of	203
artwork—more than forty sketches and color designs, to be exact! After submitting their	217
ideas, the Postal Service decided to focus on one postal theme. A second round of sketches	233
were drawn, and everyone agreed that a mailbox would be the visual element that was	248
present in all five stamps of the Looney Tunes series.	258

The Bugs Bunny Postal Stamp	263

There are many stamps with stories. For example, the popular LOVE stamp was created	277
by an artist and it has become a cultural **icon** that is directly associated with the city of	295
Philadelphia, which is known as "The City of Brotherly Love."	305
One of the most popular stamps to date is actually the Bugs Bunny stamp. In the	321
1990s, the U.S. Postal Service joined forces with Warner Brothers to put Bugs Bunny on a	337
postage stamp. However, everyone did not like this. Many collectors worried that the Bugs	351
Bunny stamp was too popular for the program and others were concerned that the cartoon	366
character would replace subjects that were important to	374
history. There was a great benefit in Bugs Bunny, though.	384
Bugs was so popular that the Postal Service used this	394
choice to encourage stamp collecting among young people.	402
Therefore, the stamp was able to satisfy a wide audience,	412
especially children.	414

glossary

icon:
Widely known as a symbol.

Words read in 1 minute – errors = WPM

CHECK FOR UNDERSTANDING

Adults: After your early achiever has finished reading, ask for a brief summary of the story so you can check comprehension. Write the summary on the lines below.

_____

_____

_____

GUIDED QUESTIONS

Use "The Art of the Postal Stamp" to answer the following questions.

1. According to the author, who determines the look of the postal stamp?

   _____

   _____

2. Reread this sentence:

   "Therefore, the stamp was able to satisfy a wide audience, **especially** children."

   How does the word **especially** help you to understand the meaning of the sentence?

   _____

   _____

3. Why were people arguing about the Bugs Bunny stamp?_____

   _____

   _____

4. Write a sentence describing the design process of the Bugs Bunny stamp.

   _____

   _____

Bare Bones: A Study Group

The following is an excerpt from a group of 4th-grade students who are preparing for a	17
quiz on the parts of a bone.	24
Lucile: Our quiz is going to be on the parts of a bone. We should study so that we are	44
prepared.	45
Kareem: Okay. Let's start by answering this question: Why is the skeletal system	58
important?	59
Arnez: That's easy. Every person has a body made up of bones, or skeletal system,	74
which gives our body structure. Our bones allow us to move in different ways and, of	90
course, they protect our organs.	95
Lucile: Our recent field trip to the museum also taught us something very important	109
about our bones. Can anyone remember?	115
Kareem: I do! We learned that our bones are alive. They may be hard and dry, but they	133
are growing and changing each day.	139
Lucile: That's correct. Almost all of our bones are made up of many layers. Kareem, do	155
you remember what those layers are?	161

Kareem: Well, I remember that the outer	168
surface is called the **periosteum** (pare-ee-	173
OS-tee-um). It is thin, but it also contains	181
nerves and blood vessels.	185
Arnez: And the next layer is known as	193
compact bone. It's smooth—the part	199
you see when you look at a skeleton.	207
The compact bone contains cancellous	212
(kan-se-les), a layer that looks like a	219
sponge. This protects the innermost part	225
of the bone, the bone marrow.	231
Lucile: Yes. Bone marrow looks like jelly!	238
But its primary job is to make blood cells.	247
We sure do know our bones! We should do	256
very well on our quiz.	261
Kareem: Make no bones about it.	267
We sure will!	270

Words read in 1 minute – errors = WPM

CHECK FOR UNDERSTANDING

Adults: After your early achiever has finished reading, ask for a brief summary of the story so you can check comprehension. Write the summary on the lines below.

_____

_____

_____

GUIDED QUESTIONS

Use "Bare Bones: A Study Group" to answer the following questions.

1. What is the main purpose of the study group?

    _____

    _____

2. Reread these sentences with expression:

    "Well, I remember that the outer surface is called the **periosteum** (pare-ee-OS-tee-um). It is thin, but it also contains nerves and blood vessels."

    What is the meaning of **periosteum**? Which other words or parts in the sentences help you to understand its meaning?

    _____

    _____

3. Which layer helps to protect the bone marrow? _____

    _____

    _____

4. What does Lucile compare bone marrow to? What does this mean?

    _____

    _____

Reading and Writing: Informational Texts

Famous Scientists

Being able to read informational passages and understand their meaning is an important quality of a successful reader.

In this section, you will read a mix of historical and scientific material. The activities will test your ability to understand the information by asking you to answer questions based on what is directly stated, as well as what may be only suggested in the texts.

Read the passage first so that you can pick out the main ideas. Look for other features such as the author's tone and point of view, as well as the organization of the passage itself. Refer back to the appropriate areas in the text as you work out each question. Using the information presented, sharpen your reasoning abilities by writing about what you learn.

Writing will help you to clarify new information by building upon what you know and what you feel to be true, or your opinion.

Dedicated to a Cure

1   When you are feeling sick, you may go to the doctor to get medicine or a type of treatment to help you feel better. Some of the medicines and treatments that doctors use today are the result of the study and efforts of people who lived before us. An outstanding person, Marie Curie, became a world-famous scientist who led the way in making important discoveries that have saved many lives.

2   Curie was born Maria Sklodowska on November 7, 1867 in Warsaw, Poland. Her father taught math and **physics** at the university there. When Marie grew up, she also wanted to study physics. Like her father, Marie was interested in the properties of matter and energy. She quickly discovered that women were not allowed to attend the University of Warsaw. In 1891, however, a determined Marie moved to France. She attended the Sorbonne, a university in Paris, where she received a degree in physics. While at school, Sklodowska met and married Pierre Curie.

3   United in their vision, the Curies worked hard. Together, their work led to the discovery of two very important elements—**polonium** and radium. Radium is a naturally occurring **radioactive** material that is still used today by doctors to treat cancer. Radioactive materials release high-energy waves (called radiation) that destroy living cells. Although Curie understood the dangers of working with radioactive materials, she continued in her lifelong mission. This discovery not only led to the treatment of cancer but it also earned the Curies the Nobel Prize for Physics in 1903.

4   A few years after the Curies won their Nobel Prize, Pierre Curie passed away. Following the death of her husband, Curie was very sad but she continued her work. Curie took over her husband's job, becoming the first female **professor** at the University of Paris. In 1911, she received her second Nobel Prize in Chemistry for her work with radium and for creating the word *radioactivity*.

5   Curie truly cared for people. During World War I, she worked hard to ease soldiers' pain and suffering. She believed X-rays would help doctors find bullets and metal inside of the bodies of injured soldiers. However, moving hurt soldiers could be dangerous because of their condition. Therefore, she developed X-ray vans so that these soldiers would not have to be moved to receive an X-ray.

6   Marie Curie oversaw the building of a center named in her honor. The center's mission was to find a cure for cancer. In 1923, the Marie Sklodowska Curie **Oncology** Center was opened. At the opening ceremony, she donated a gram of radium, which had been funded by Polish women's groups from Canada and the United States.

7   In 1934, Curie passed away due to a blood disease from the years of working with radioactive materials. Curie will always be remembered as a **pioneer** in the study of radiation, a treatment method used by doctors today to help treat cancer patients.

glossary

oncology: The study of cancers and tumors.

polonium: Silver-colored radioactive metal from the radioactive breakdown of uranium.

radioactive: Having or producing a powerful and dangerous form of energy, called radiation.

FINDING MAIN IDEAS AND DETAILS

Use "Dedicated to a Cure" to answer the following questions.

1. What is the **main idea** of the article?

   A. Curie's work helped in the development of medical X-ray vans.

   B. Curie was the first woman professor to teach at a famous university in France.

   C. Proper guidelines should be followed when working with radioactive materials.

   D. Curie was a famous scientist whose work improved medicine and saved the lives of many people.

2. Which sentence **best** supports the main idea of the article?

   A. "Curie was born Maria Sklodowska on November 7, 1867 in Warsaw, Poland."

   B. "This discovery not only led to the treatment of cancer but it also earned the Curies the Nobel Prize for Physics in 1903."

   C. "Curie took over her husband's job, becoming the first female professor at the University of Paris."

   D. "At the opening ceremony, she donated a gram of radium, which had been funded by Polish women's groups from Canada and the United States."

3. Why do you think Marie Curie continued to work with radioactive materials even though she knew they were dangerous? Gather information from the text to figure out the answer. Remember to use quotation marks if you cite sentences directly from the text.

   _____

   _____

   _____

4. Which sentence is **most** important to include in a **summary** of this article?

   A. "Together, their work led to the discovery of two very important elements—polonium and radium."

   B. "During World War I, she worked hard to ease soldiers' pain and suffering."

   C. "Although Curie understood the dangers of working with radioactive materials, she continued in her lifelong mission."

   D. "Radioactive materials release high-energy waves (called radiation) that destroy living cells."

Reading and Writing: Informational Texts

Review the timeline of events in Marie Curie's life. Can you keep track of the important dates and events that occurred in Marie Curie's life? How does this affect your understanding of the text? Answer the questions that follow.

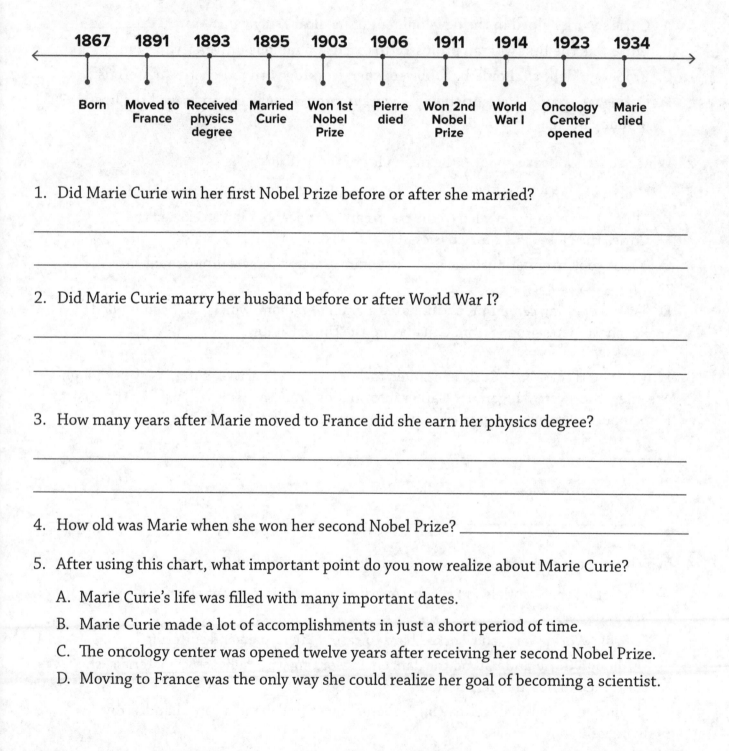

1867	1891	1893	1895	1903	1906	1911	1914	1923	1934
Born	Moved to France	Received physics degree	Married Curie	Won 1st Nobel Prize	Pierre died	Won 2nd Nobel Prize	World War I	Oncology Center opened	Marie died

1. Did Marie Curie win her first Nobel Prize before or after she married?

_____

_____

2. Did Marie Curie marry her husband before or after World War I?

_____

_____

3. How many years after Marie moved to France did she earn her physics degree?

_____

_____

4. How old was Marie when she won her second Nobel Prize? _____

5. After using this chart, what important point do you now realize about Marie Curie?

   A. Marie Curie's life was filled with many important dates.

   B. Marie Curie made a lot of accomplishments in just a short period of time.

   C. The oncology center was opened twelve years after receiving her second Nobel Prize.

   D. Moving to France was the only way she could realize her goal of becoming a scientist.

UNDERSTANDING THE CLUES

You can understand the meaning of an unknown word by looking at the surrounding words and sentences. These are called **context clues**.

Example: **Question:** What does the word **hypothesis** mean?

The geologist had never seen that type of reaction before. Using his **background knowledge**, he made a hypothesis to explain the events that occurred.

Answer: "Using the clue words background knowledge, I figured that a hypothesis is a smart guess based on information the geologist already knew."

Use "Dedicated to a Cure" to answer the following questions.

1. Which choice best describes the word **physics** in the sentence below? Use clues from the story to help you understand.

   *"When Marie grew up, she also wanted to study **physics**."*

   A. The study of medical treatments.

   B. The study of matter and energy.

   C. The study of chemical treatments.

   D. The study of medicine and energy.

2. Read the following sentence from the text.

   *"Curie will always be remembered as a **pioneer** in the study of radiation, a treatment method used by doctors today to help cancer patients."*

   What does the word **pioneer** mean in the context of this sentence?

   A. A person who raises awareness of a cause.

   B. A person who leads the way for a specific cause.

   C. A person who studies the treatment of cancer.

   D. A person who helps other people during their sickness.

3. Read the following sentence from the text. *"Curie took over her husband's job, becoming the first female **professor** at the University of Paris."*

Which of the following **best** describes the meaning of the word **professor**?

A. scientist

B. inventor

C. teacher

D. researcher

USING RELATIVE PRONOUNS

Relative pronouns such as ***whose, whom, who, which***, and ***that*** are used to connect a phrase to a noun or a pronoun. Relative pronouns are usually found at the beginning of an adjective clause because they introduce it. An adjective clause is a group of words with a subject that provide a description.

- *Whom* and *who* are used to refer to people.
- *Which* is used to refer to things.
- *That* and *whose* refer to people, things, ideas, or qualities.

A relative pronoun begins an adjective clause to identify the noun.

Example 1: We learned about the element <u>that</u> Marie had discovered.

The noun being identified is the element.

A relative pronoun begins an adjective clause to provide more information about the noun.

Example 2: Marie, <u>who</u> discovered radium, studied hard in physics class.

The noun is Marie. The adjective clause tells more about her.

Circle the relative pronoun that *best* completes the sentence.

1. Did you see (who, whom) the winner of the science fair was?

2. Alexis, (who, whose) husband was a scientist, was awarded the Nobel Prize.

3. The chemistry class, (which, whose) was full, had over fifty students.

4. The university (where, whose, that) she teaches physics is in France.

PROGRESSIVE VERB TENSES

A verb changes its form to show the time of an event, condition, or action. The progressive verb tense describes ongoing actions in the present, past, and future.

> **Progressive Tense**
>
> **Present**   am/is/are experimenting
>
> **Past**   was/were experimenting
>
> **Future**   will be experimenting
>
> 1. I **am** experimenting in my lab
> 2. He **was** experimenting in my lab.
> 3. She **will be** experimenting in my lab.

Complete each sentence by changing the verb in parentheses to the tense indicated.

1. The group of scientists _____ by 7:00 p.m.   (future progressive, **arrive**)

2. My brother _____ his chemistry homework.   (past progressive, **finish**)

3. The students _____ for their physics test.   (future progressive, **study**)

4. Researchers _____ for a cure for cancer.   (present progressive, **search**)

Challenge: Research other inventors and inventions. Write a paragraph about another invention that changed the world for the better. Use past progressive sentences and include a few relative pronouns.

_____

_____

_____

_____

_____

_____

An Unusual Mind

1   Do you think in pictures rather than words? Have you ever imagined walking on the clouds or riding along a beam of light? A young boy named Albert Einstein thought this way. As he got older, he made many important discoveries through visual experiments that he performed in his mind, known as thought experiments. Einstein's discoveries redefined the world of science and made him one of the most famous scientists in history.

2   Albert Einstein was born in Ulm, Germany on March 14, 1879. As a young boy, his parents took him to a doctor because they were worried when he did not speak as early as other children his age. Although this caused concern, being late to use verbal communication actually helped make Einstein a **genius**. Since his language development was slow, he thought in pictures rather than words. He became curious about other things, such as space and time. At age five, his father gave him a compass, which awakened his curiosity about the Earth's magnetic field. As a result, this sparked the scientific journey to which he dedicated his life.

3   In 1905 Albert Einstein became famous. Scientists around the world were talking about his ideas. During his "miracle" year, Einstein wrote four papers that **revolutionized** physics, introducing new concepts of time and space, and changed the way scientists viewed the universe. One of his greatest discoveries was called the *Theory of Relativity*. Einstein's belief stated that it is impossible to know if you are moving without looking at another object. It also states that the speed of light is **constant** or steady and that nothing moves faster than light. This **theory** changed what scientists believed about gravity and the force of attraction between two objects, pulling objects together like magnets.

4   Although many scientists did not agree with Einstein's Theory of Relativity, it was finally proved in 1919. A few years later, in 1922, Einstein was awarded the 1921 Nobel Prize for Physics because his discovery was so very important to many areas of science. In the eyes of many, Einstein was a genius, one of the smartest people who ever lived. His legacy, discoveries, and research continue to mold and shape the scientific world today.

MAPPING THE MAIN IDEA AND SUPPORTING DETAILS

Using "An Unusual Mind," complete the graphic organizer below by stating the main idea and supporting details.

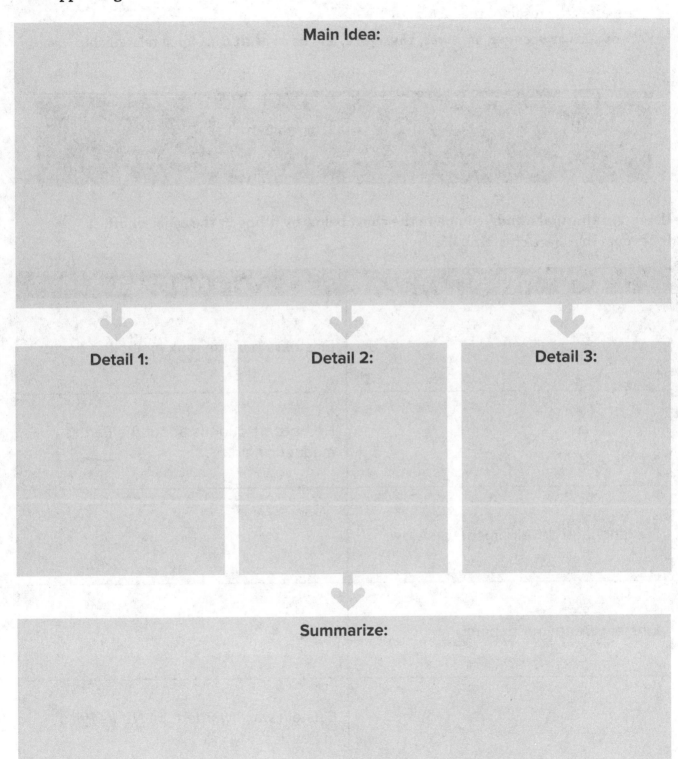

Main Idea:

Detail 1:

Detail 2:

Detail 3:

Summarize:

Reading and Writing: Informational Texts

UNDERSTANDING CAUSE AND EFFECT

The connection between some ideas and concepts can be expressed as a *cause and effect*.

- A *cause* is an action that makes something happen.
- An *effect* is the result of that action.
- Words such as **because**, **so**, **since, therefore**, and **as a result** can signal relationship.

> Example: The scientist is famous (**effect**). He discovered a new planet (**cause**).
>
> The scientist is famous **because** he discovered a new planet.

Using "An Unusual Mind," complete the chart below by filling in the cause or effect for events in Albert Einstein's life.

CAUSE	EFFECT
	Einstein's parents took him to the doctor.
	He became curious about the Earth's magnetic field.
His language development was slow.	
Einstein wrote four papers.	
	Einstein was awarded the Nobel Prize in Physics.

UNDERSTANDING THE CLUES

Clues within the text can help you determine the meaning of an unknown word.

> Example: Kaylee did not win the science fair, but her efforts were ***acknowledged*** when she was given a purple ribbon.
>
> **Question:** What does <u>acknowledged</u> mean?
>
> **Clue:** (*Think*) Kaylee was given a purple ribbon so she could be <u>recognized</u> for her work.
>
> **Answer:** <u>Acknowledged</u> means to be recognized.

Use "An Unusual Mind" to answer the following questions.

1. Which word best describes **theory** as used in the article?

   A. experiment
   B. famous
   C. invention
   D. belief

2. Reread paragraph 3. Which of the following is a context clue that can help you understand the meaning of the word **constant**?

   A. steady
   B. faster
   C. light
   D. speed

3. Which of the following answers best describes a **genius**? Use clues from the story to help you understand.

   A. Someone who has a very good theory.
   B. A person who is very intelligent.
   C. A person who uses thought experiments.
   D. Someone who is a well-known scientist.

4. Write the context clues from the article that help to describe the word **revolutionize**. Then, write the meaning of the word.

   _____

   _____

HELPING VERBS

Auxiliary verbs, also known as helping verbs, such as **will**, **shall**, **may**, **might**, **can**, **could**, **must**, **ought to**, **should**, **would**, **used to**, and **need**, are used to show the time or mood of a main verb. When you combine helping verbs with main verbs, you create what is known as a **verb phrase**.

Example 1: Nigel **may** become a scientist.

In this example "may" is used to express the possibility of Nigel becoming a scientist in the future.

Example 2: **May** I go to school to become a scientist?

In this example "may" is used to ask permission to go to school to become a scientist. "Might" is used to express possibility—but usually a much smaller possibility than "may" expresses.

Example 3: I **might** become a scientist someday, but I doubt it.

Activity 1

Write four sentences on the lines that correctly use the helping verbs _may_ or _might_.

1. _____

2. _____

3. _____

4. _____

Activity 2

Underline the helping verb that correctly completes each sentence.

1. My report on Albert Einstein absolutely (may, might, must) be ready tomorrow, so I need to get to the library tonight.

2. Jaden (could, must, shall) have passed his science test easily if only he'd spent a bit more time studying.

3. Leia (used to, would, will) be here any minute; she just went to drop off her science project.

WRITE YOUR OPINION

Albert Einstein's research and discoveries revolutionized the way scientists viewed the universe. He touched on important concepts and redefined many things that scientists thought were true. Do you think that Einstein was truly the smartest scientist in history? Why do you think Einstein was able to have such an effect on the scientific community? What made him so special?

Write an essay stating your answer. Use evidence from the text to support your opinion. You can also do a little more research on Einstein with the help of an adult. Be sure your essay has a topic sentence, or main idea, that tells your opinion. Next, list three reasons why you believe, or do not believe, that Einstein is the smartest scientist in history. Remember to cite evidence from the text. Finally, write a conclusion that restates your opinion. Use the graphic organizer below to help you plan your essay.

Topic sentence: _____

_____

_____

Reason 1: _____

_____

_____

Reason 2: _____

_____

_____

Reason 3: _____

_____

_____

Conclusion: _____

_____

_____

Famous Artists and Composers

An artist becomes famous for a special style or for the effect the person's artwork has on other people. Throughout Europe, from about 1350–1650 C.E., there was new growth and fresh change in music and the fine arts that was called the Renaissance. More artists emerged from various countries and regions and produced musical and artistic styles never before heard or seen. The value of creating and learning went to a higher level, and people had a newfound respect for the arts. Some sculptors, painters, and composers became world-famous, and their work was recognized as brilliant during their lifetime and beyond. Today, artists have followed in their footsteps, often using techniques from these earlier artists to create a unique style all of their own.

Ludwig van Beethoven: A Heart for Music

1   This is the story of a remarkable man named Ludwig van Beethoven, who became deaf. He did not let the loss of hearing affect his ability to compose beautiful music. Some of his most famous works were created after he became deaf. Ludwig van Beethoven is considered to be one of the greatest **composers** who ever lived.

2   Beethoven became a musical genius at an early age. When he was only seven years old, he performed his first public concert. He learned to play the organ and how to compose music from renowned musician Gottlob Neefe. Just before age 12, he published his very first composition. In 1783, Neefe was so impressed with Beethoven that he said of him in the *Magazine of Music,* "If he continues like this, he will be, without a doubt, the new Mozart." In fact, by the time he was just 16 years old in 1787, Beethoven traveled to Vienna, Austria, to study music with Wolfgang Amadeus Mozart.

3   Beethoven was quite stubborn and did not play the same way as other musicians of his time. He would often improvise, or make up the notes, as he went along. Beethoven's work had strong emotion. He often composed about the things he loved the most, such as nature and social justice.

4   In 1801, Beethoven began to lose his hearing. A year later in 1802, he was so saddened by this that he wrote a famous text expressing **sorrow** about the unfairness of life—why should he, a composer, lose his hearing? He was so upset that he lost his desire to live. However, his passion for his work carried him through this tough time. Despite his increasing hearing loss, he felt that he had much more to do. As a result, he focused all of his energy in making music and absorbed himself into creating new works. During this time, he created some of the most beautiful and powerful pieces of his career. Beethoven's *Symphony No. 3*, later renamed the *Eroica Symphony*, was one of his most outstanding and **original** works. In this **symphony,** Beethoven played the piano using broad strokes of sound to tell his audience how he felt about life and being alive. This kind of music had never been played before. Therefore, it changed people's understanding of what a symphony could be. This masterpiece was so great and different from anything anyone had ever heard that the musicians could not learn how to play it, despite weeks of practice.

5   During his last ten years of life, when Beethoven was completely deaf, he developed some of the greatest music ever written—music that truly came from his heart. A few of his late works include *Missa Solemnis* and *String Quartet No. 14.* In 1824, he completed his ninth, and last, symphony, which is perhaps the most famous piece of music in history. *The Ninth Symphony* was born from Beethoven's desire for freedom. He was deeply disturbed by the ruling monarchs in Europe at the time, which prevented people from living life with liberty and peace. This symphony was a symbol of his desire for the freedoms that every human wants—political freedom, freedom of expression, and freedom of mind and spirit.

FINDING MAIN IDEAS AND DETAILS

Use "Ludwig van Beethoven: A Heart for Music" to answer the following questions.

1. What is the **main idea** of the article?

    A. Beethoven was the youngest musician in history.

    B. Beethoven was one of the greatest composers in the world.

    C. Beethoven's music was so original, musicians could not play it.

    D. Beethoven created his best music after he became deaf.

2. Which sentence provides the **best** supporting detail for the main idea of the article?

    A. Beethoven took music lessons from other famous composers.

    B. Beethoven often improvised, or made up notes, as he went along.

    C. He did not let the loss of hearing affect his ability to compose music.

    D. In 1787, Beethoven traveled to Austria to take music lessons from Mozart.

3. The article does not directly say this, but Wolfgang Amadeus Mozart was also an amazing composer and a world-famous musician. What evidence from the text supports this conclusion?

    _____

    _____

    _____

4. As you review the events in the life of Beethoven, what important lesson can you learn? How can you apply this principle in your life?

    _____

    _____

    _____

Digging Deeper

The Musician in You!
What type of music do you like to sing along to? Write your own song lyrics and then share with others.

RELATIONSHIPS BETWEEN EVENTS

1. What early events from Beethoven's life show that he had a special talent for music? List at least two events.

   _____

   _____

2. What was the turning point in Beethoven's life?

   A. When he published his first composition.

   B. When he realized he was becoming deaf.

   C. When he took music lessons from famous composer Gottlob Neefe.

   D. When he took music lessons from Wolfgang Amadeus Mozart.

3. What events led up to the development of the *Eroica Symphony*?

   _____

   _____

4. What effect did the *Eroica Symphony* have on the music community at that time?

   _____

   _____

5. What moved Beethoven to create his *Ninth Symphony*? Circle all that apply.

   A. He wanted political freedom.

   B. He wanted to create another masterpiece.

   C. He wanted Europe's monarchs to expand their rule.

   D. He wanted to create a symbol of freedom for people to enjoy.

   E. He wanted to express and play the kind of music that he felt was important.

VOCABULARY DEVELOPMENT AND USE

Use "Ludwig van Beethoven: A Heart for Music" to answer the following questions.

1. Which choice is the best meaning of the word **composer** in paragraph 1?

   A. A person who makes money playing the piano.

   B. A person who makes money playing the violin and the piano.

   C. A person who makes money performing in public concerts.

   D. A person who makes money writing and playing their own music.

2. Read this sentence from the text.

   *"A year later in 1802, he was so saddened by this that he wrote a famous text expressing **sorrow** about the unfairness of life—why should he, a composer, lose his hearing?"*

   Which word would best replace the word **sorrow** in the sentence above?

   A. feeling

   B. thoughts

   C. sadness

   D. confusion

3. Read paragraphs 4 and 5. Explain the meaning of the word **symphony**. What clues help you know this?

   _____

   _____

4. Read this sentence from the article.

   *"Beethoven's Symphony No. 3, later renamed the Eroica Symphony, was one of his most outstanding and **original** works."*

   What is the best meaning of the word **original** as used in the sentence above?

   A. A work that is very popular.

   B. A work that is not accepted.

   C. A work that is similar to another work.

   D. A work that is different from other works.

PREPOSITIONAL PHRASES

Prepositional phrases connect nouns or pronouns to the rest of the sentence and end with an object. The object is usually the noun or pronoun. They also add meaning to nouns and verbs in sentences.

Prepositions are words such as *in, near, over, past, about, above, across, up,* and *upon*. Prepositional phrases provide more information about who, why, what, where, or how. Finding and using prepositional phrases makes a piece of writing more interesting.

Example: Angelique saw a group of musicians playing a piano on the sidewalk.

The prepositional phrase is "**on the sidewalk**." The preposition is "**on**" and the direct object is "**sidewalk**."

Activity 1

Read the sentences below. Underline the prepositional phrases, draw a box around the preposition, and circle the direct objects in the paragraph. Some sentences may have more than one prepositional phrase, preposition, and direct object.

1. The fan blew the music sheet under the piano during the concert.

2. After our big concert, Zach and I left the auditorium with them.

3. Beethoven lived and worked in Vienna, Austria, for most of his life.

4. By the time Beethoven was seven, he was performing in public places.

Activity 2

Now create four sentences that contain prepositional phrases using one or more prepositions from the word bank.

1. _____

2. _____

3. _____

4. _____

word bank

outside

past

around

between

down

up

without

from

toward

until

CLARIFYING COMMONLY CONFUSED WORDS

There are many words in written language that can be easily confused. Words that sound alike, or nearly alike, but have different meanings are often confusing. Some of the most common ones are words like "too" and "to" or "there," "their," and "they're."

> Example: My mother bought (to, two, too) violins at the garage sale.
>
> **Correct Answer:** Two

Underline the correct word(s) that complete each sentence.

1. Zachary is going to (write, right) his own music for the school play.

2. Our music teacher has (to, two, too) many music books, so she is giving some of them (to, two, too) her students.

3. Mother (allowed, aloud) sister to play the piano if she promised not to (break, brake) it.

4. My parents bought (hour, our) grandparents a brand new piano for (there, their, they're) anniversary.

5. Josh's parents are paying for guitar lessons because (they're, their, there) musicians.

CHOOSING PUNCTUATION FOR EFFECT

Punctuation gives meaning to written words the same way tones and sounds give meaning to a spoken word. You can express the feeling and tone of the information you write with proper use of punctuation. A mistake in punctuation can change the whole meaning of a thought or sentence.

Here are some examples:

1. Use **parentheses** ( ) to group together information that makes a thought more clear or is used as an afterthought. Using parentheses shows that the writer considered the information less important.

   Janet said that she finished all of her art homework **(12 pages)** in one night.

   My music teacher loves to teach **(and read biographies)** about famous Renaissance composers.

2. **Commas and exclamation marks** are used to offset *interjections* (e.g., *yes, indeed, absolutely*). Interjections are words or phrases that express emotions and are included in a sentence to express different feelings such as surprise, disgust, or excitement. You might use an interjection to express surprise (Wow!), confusion (Huh?), or anger (No!).

   No, he composed the *Eroica Symphony*.

   Indeed, it was the best musical piece in history.

   Wow! Arthur said that he could create ten songs each day!

3. **Dashes** add emphasis, interrupt, or show an abrupt change of thought.

   Beethoven was the one, the only composer, whose music moved me to learn the piano.

   Beethoven was the one—the only composer—whose music moved me to learn the piano.

   I clean up the mess; my little brother just plays all day.

   I clean up the mess—my little brother just plays all day.

Activity 1

Add parentheses where appropriate in the following sentences.

1. I remembered the entire musical poem it was not easy and recited it for my class.

2. Did you get your permission slip the pink one for the music museum trip tomorrow?

3. Be sure to read both music articles 7 pages each before you take the test.

4. Some kids do not like music history but all my life I have loved the piano.

5. We have to compose our own songs simple ones for our music class project.

Activity 2

Add commas or exclamation marks after the interjections and dashes where necessary.

1. Yes my mother will come on our class trip tomorrow.

2. There is so much to learn about the Renaissance period I can't wait to go on the trip tomorrow.

3. Good I was hoping that we would go on a field trip this month.

4. Uh Oh Sharon forgot to bring in her signed permission slip.

5. The museum trip will be a lot of fun in fact we will be taking two tours.

Activity 3

Read the paragraph below. Place proper punctuation marks where they belong. Insert parentheses, commas, dashes, and exclamation marks.

My sister Syntisha's music class went on a field trip. They went to the New Music Museum. Thankfully they had a wonderful tour guide, Mr. Deepak. Syntisha said it was the best tour she ever had the worst one was last year at the planetarium. Her class decided to take the 1950s Music Tour she loves Elvis and the Music History Tour it had a brand new section for young artists. The teacher gave a challenge to the class. She said, "Whoever takes the best notes complete notes and emails them to me tonight will win a free homework pass." Wow what a cool teacher Syntisha has! My sister took a lot of notes. When she got home, she sent an email to her teacher. *"Mrs. Chin, thank you for taking us to the museum today. Here are the notes I took see attachment I hope you like them. Wow I learned a lot of great things today. It was fun! See you in class tomorrow. Sincerely, Syntisha."*

WRITE YOUR RESEARCH REPORT

Researching to Build Knowledge: Investigate the Renaissance Era. What was this period in history and why was it so important? What other famous composers or artists became famous during this time? Use the Internet or other sources to perform your research. Use evidence from the text as well as additional print (magazines, newspapers, books) or Internet research on the subject. When using the Internet, make sure to use credible websites, such as education websites (.edu), government websites (.gov), nonprofit websites (.org), or other teacher-approved sites.

Collect information, organize the information, and then develop your report. Create a works cited page to list all of the sources you used.

Topic: _____

Main point #1: _____

Subpoint: _____

Subpoint: _____

Subpoint: _____

Main point #2: _____

Subpoint: _____

Subpoint: _____

Subpoint: _____

Main point #3: _____

Subpoint: _____

Subpoint: _____

Conclusion: _____

_____

Works cited: _____

REVIEW

Congratulations! You have completed the lessons in this section. Now you will have the chance to practice some of the skills you just learned.

Reading Fluency

Adults: Time your student reading aloud for one minute, and cross out any words that were eliminated or misread. At the end of one minute, mark the last word read and allow your student to finish reading the text. (Your student should be able to read 110–140 words per minute.) Count the total number of errors and subtract that from the number of words read. This will give you the total number of words read per minute.

Charles Schulz—The Cartoonist

"Charlie Brown," "Snoopy," "Linus," and "Peppermint Patty" are famous characters who 11
make up the gang of the comic series *Peanuts. Peanuts* is one of the most popular comic 28
strips in history, written and illustrated by well-known **cartoonist** Charles M. Schulz. 40

Charles M. Schulz was born an only child to Dena and Carl Schulz on November 26, 55
1922. Schulz's life as a future cartoonist began just two days after he was born, when his 72
uncle nicknamed him "Sparky," after the horse from the *Barney Google* comic strip. 85

Charles and his father spent their Sunday mornings reading the funnies in the 98
newspaper. He loved the *Mickey Mouse, Skippy,* and *Popeye* comic strips. These comic 111
strips inspired the young boy to become a cartoonist. In 1937, when he was only fifteen 127
years old, his first cartoon was published in the "Ripley's Believe It or Not" daily cartoon. 143
The cartoon featured "Spike," the Schulz's family dog. 151

After high school, Schulz went to college to pursue his dream as a cartoonist until 1943, 167
when two important events happened that affected the rest of his life. Schulz's mother, 181
whom he loved dearly, died of cancer at the age of fifty. Within days of this event, he was 200
on a train to Kentucky to fight in World War II. His dreams of becoming a cartoonist were 218
put on hold. 221

Two years later, he was discharged from the army. Schulz's career as a cartoonist came 236
about in 1947, when he created a comic strip called *L'il Folks,* that appeared each week in 253
The Saturday Evening Post. The cartoon was created with drawings of children with large 267
heads, who used words and actions well above their age. 277

In 1950, the *Peanuts* gang was born. This cartoon, with encouraging messages and 290
helpful life lessons, ran for fifty years in over 2,600 newspapers in seventy-five different 304
countries. Through Schulz's **humor** and silliness, he was able to keep his characters fresh 318

enough to keep his audience coming   324
back for more. Schulz received many   330
awards for his cartoon specials that   336
aired on television. The *Peanuts* gang   342
continues to bring laughter to many   348
people today.   350

Words read in 1 minute – errors = WPM

Activity 1

Use what you know about relative pronouns to underline the word that best completes each sentence.

1. Charlie Brown, (who, whose) best friend was Linus, had a dog named Snoopy.

2. Charles Schulz, (who, whom, that) wrote the *Peanuts* comic strip, was in World War II.

Activity 2

Rewrite each sentence using the proper progressive tense.

1. Jeffraisha Hudson is creating a children's comic strip about a lion and a mouse.

   (create, future progressive) _____

   _____

2. The cartoonist is drawing pictures for *The Lion and the Mouse,* an animated movie.

   (draw, past progressive) _____

   _____

Activity 3

Use what you know about helping verbs to underline the verb that correctly completes each sentence.

1. The comic strip (must, has, should) come out in *The Sunday Register*
   if Calvin finishes it on time.

2. (Shall, Would, Will) I help you draw the pictures for the comic strip?

Activity 4

Use what you know about prepositional phrases to write three sentences that contain prepositional phrases using the prepositions around, after, and between.

1. _____

2. _____

3. _____

Activity 5

Use what you know about commonly confused words to write three sentences using the correct form of to, two, and too.

1. _____

2. _____

3. _____

Activity 6

Use what you know about using punctuation for effect by adding commas, dashes, parentheses, or exclamation points where needed.

1. Whoopie My dad gave me the Sunday paper so I can read the comics.

2. Will you read me the cartoon strip found below of Snoopy?

Activity 7

Use what you know about using context clues to find the meaning of unknown words to answer these questions.

1. Explain what a **cartoonist** is. _____

_____

2. Which word in the article is a context clue for the word **humor**? _____

Read the following article. Use what you learned from the units to answer the questions below.

Dr. Seuss

1 With his memorable rhymes, funny characters, and witty words, Dr. Seuss has become one of the most famous children's book authors in the world.

2 American writer, poet, and cartoonist, Dr. Seuss was born Theodor Seuss Geisel on March 2, 1904 in Springfield, Massachusetts. As a young boy, Geisel's mother often put him to sleep with rhymes from her own childhood. He credits his mother for his great ability to create rhymes. **Illustrations** in many of Geisel's books reflect his childhood memories.

3 Geisel began his career as a cartoonist at the beginning of World War II, working for a magazine creating political cartoons. He also worked for the U.S. Army, making movies to help train soldiers. During the war, publishers saw his work and asked him to draw pictures for a children's book. As a result of this experience, Geisel wanted to write his own children's book.

4 Geisel loved writing for children. He often put on silly hats to help create a mood so that he could finish his stories. His first book, *And to Think That I Saw It on Mulberry Street*, almost did not get published. Publishers rejected the book twenty-seven times. However, in 1937, Vanguard Press decided to publish the book. When Geisel's first book hit the market, it changed the world of children's literature. In 1957, his popular series, *The Cat in the Hat*, made him famous. The story, which was only 236 words long, with funny illustrations and playful rhymes, became one of the best-selling series Beginner Books to teach children how to read.

5 Geisel has written and illustrated forty-four children's books and sold over half a billion copies. His most popular books include *Green Eggs and Ham*, *How the Grinch Stole Christmas*, and *Fox in Socks*. Dr. Seuss has won many awards throughout his career. Even after his death in 1991, Dr. Seuss continues to be one of the best-selling children's book authors in the world.

Activity 1

Use "Dr. Seuss" to answer the following questions.

1. In the space below, write the **main idea** of the article.

   _____

   _____

2. List **three details** that support the main idea of the article.

   _____

   _____

   _____

3. Reread paragraph 2. What does the word **illustration** mean?

   A. words

   B. rhymes

   C. pictures

   D. books

4. How did Dr. Seuss's mother help him become a successful author? _____

   _____

   _____

Activity 2   Use the chart below to answer the following questions.

AWARD	YEAR	BOOK
Caldecott Honor Award	1947	*McElligot's Pool*
Caldecott Honor Award	1949	*Bartholomew and the Oobleck*
Caldecott Honor Award	1950	*If I Ran the Zoo*
Laura Ingalls Wilder Award	1980	*If I Ran the Zoo*
New York Library Lion	1986	*McElligot's Pool*

1. Dr. Seuss won two awards for which book titles?

    _____

    _____

2. In what year did *Bartholomew and the Oobleck* win an award?

    _____

    _____

DISCOVER

Write Your Opinion

Think about the famous scientists, artists, composers, and authors you have read about in this unit. What is a common theme that you can find among some of these articles? Did any of these people have challenges to overcome?

Write your opinion, stating which famous person you admire the most. Why do you admire this person? Use evidence from any of the articles to support your views. Write an opinion essay stating your answer. Be sure your essay has a topic sentence (or main idea) that tells your opinion. Next, list three reasons why you admire this person. Finally, write a conclusion that restates your opinion. Use the graphic organizer below to help you plan your essay.

Topic Sentence:

_____

_____

Reason 1:

_____

_____

_____

Reason 2:

_____

_____

_____

Reason 3:

_____

_____

_____

Conclusion:

_____

_____

_____

_____

On the Road to Discovery and Innovation

Take an exciting adventure as you read about interesting developments in science and technology. Whether it is unique weather patterns that produce one of the world's most precious stones or a husband and wife team that developed a system of roadways to greatly improve life for every person living in the United States, it is important to remember that great discoveries are the result of new ways of thinking about what you already know.

Diamond Rain

1   If you looked outside your window one day and saw that it was raining diamonds instead of water, what would you think? That would be almost impossible, wouldn't it? Well, scientists have discovered that diamond rain actually happens on the planets of Saturn and Jupiter. Imagine that! What might be causing this unusual event?

2   Before we answer that question, let's think about why diamonds are so special. Made up of the element of **carbon**, a diamond is one of the hardest naturally occurring minerals in the world. This, along with its brilliant **luster**, makes it the perfect gemstone. Diamonds are very popular and are used to make beautiful pieces of jewelry. Not only do they make pretty rings and necklaces, they are also very important to the nation's **economy**, because companies that mine and produce diamonds are able to provide jobs for many people.

3   On Earth, scientists say it takes billions of years of strong heat and **pressure** for diamonds to form. Deep volcanic eruptions often bring diamonds to the Earth's surface.

4   However, on Jupiter and Saturn, new research shows that there are diamond mines in their skies. Scientists believe that Saturn's **atmosphere** produces nearly 2.2 million pounds of diamonds every year, with Jupiter's atmosphere also producing large amounts of diamonds. Jupiter and Saturn are made almost entirely of **helium** and **hydrogen** gas. As a result, they have the perfect temperature and pressure conditions to form diamonds.

5   How do diamonds form on these planets? Diamond rain on Jupiter and Saturn begins when lightning strikes methane, turning it into soot (carbon). Next, pressure increases when the soot falls and it becomes graphite. Afterward, the graphite falls for around 4,000 miles, increasing in pressure until it turns into a diamond. The diamonds continue to fall for thousands of miles until they reach the planet's core. However, during this phase, the temperature and pressure are so high scientists believe the diamonds may turn back into liquid carbon.

6   Scientists would like to collect the diamonds from these planets, but they believe the diamonds are in hard-to-reach areas deep inside of the planets, where the pressure is very

glossary

helium: A colorless gas that is lighter than air and is often used to fill balloons.

hydrogen: A common element that is colorless, odorless, and very light.

luster: A shine or sheen usually from reflected light.

NASA: National Aeronautics and Space Administration. A government agency set up to explore aviation and space.

great. Spacecrafts are unable to go deep enough to explore the regions and detect changes in density. However, on July 4, 2016, **NASA** sent the *Juno* spacecraft to Jupiter and Saturn to collect information on the planets' gravity and magnetic fields.

FINDING MAIN IDEAS AND DETAILS

Use "Diamond Rain" to answer the following questions.

1. What is the **main idea** of the article?

   A. Jupiter's and Saturn's atmospheres are producing large amounts of diamonds.

   B. Diamonds are one of the hardest naturally occurring minerals in the world.

   C. Volcanic eruptions often bring diamonds to the surface of the Earth.

   D. NASA plans to send Juno to explore Jupiter's and Saturn's gravity and magnetic fields.

2. Which of the following is another good title for the article?

   A. Gas Planets: Jupiter and Saturn

   B. Gas Planets: Producing Valuable Gemstones

   C. Diamonds: The Perfect Gemstone

   D. Diamond Mines: Creating Many Jobs

3. Which **key detail** supports the main idea of the article?

   A. "Deep volcanic eruptions often bring diamonds to the Earth's surface."

   B. "Not only do they make pretty rings and necklaces, they are also very important to the nation's economy."

   C. "On Earth, scientists say it takes billions of years of strong heat and pressure for diamonds to form."

   D. "However, on Jupiter and Saturn, new research shows that there are diamond mines in their skies."

Digging Deeper

Growing Crystals

Did you know that you can "grow" crystals? Crystals look much like diamonds, and they are easy to get because they are all around us. With an adult, visit your local library to look for a book about crystals and how to make them at home.

EXPLAINING STEPS IN A PROCESS

1. What is the first step in the process of diamond rain?

   A. Pressure increases when the soot falls.
   B. Graphite falls, turning into a diamond.
   C. Diamonds fall to the planet's core.
   D. Lightning strikes methane.

2. What is the next step in the process of diamond rain?

   A. Lightning strikes, turning it into soot (carbon).
   B. Soot falls, turning into graphite.
   C. The graphite becomes a diamond.
   D. The diamonds turn back into liquid carbon.

3. Lastly, explain what happens next that leads to the formation of the diamond.

An author can choose different ways to develop a text.

- Sometimes authors will develop an article in **chronological order**, or in the exact sequence of events as something happened.

- The author may present a **question** in the beginning of the text and **answer** the question at the end of the text.

- The author may choose to discuss a **problem** and then present the **solution** to the problem.

- Sometimes an author will **compare** and **contrast** information, concepts, or events within an article.

UNDERSTANDING TEXT STRUCTURE

1. How is the article, "Diamond Rain," **mainly structured**?

   A. problem and solution
   B. chronological order
   C. compare and contrast
   D. cause and effect

2. Read this excerpt from the article.

"Scientists believe that Saturn's atmosphere produces nearly 2.2 million pounds of diamonds every year, with Jupiter's atmosphere also producing large amounts of diamonds. Jupiter and Saturn are made almost entirely of helium and hydrogen gas. As a result, they have the perfect temperature and pressure conditions to form diamonds."

Which statement best describes the relationship between these sentences?

A. The sentences make a comparison.

B. The sentences describe two steps in a process.

C. The first sentence explains the reason for the second.

D. The second sentence gives the cause of the first sentence.

VOCABULARY DEVELOPMENT AND USE

Use "Diamond Rain" to answer the following questions.

You can determine the meaning of a word by looking at the surrounding words and sentences. They are clues to help you figure out its meaning.

1. What is the meaning of **atmosphere** in paragraph 4?

A. A mass of gas that surrounds a planet

B. A mass of water that surrounds a planet

C. A mass of rock that surrounds a planet

D. A mass of pressure that surrounds a planet

2. Which choice is the best meaning for the word **pressure** in paragraph 3?

A. force

B. weight

C. heat

D. load

3. Read this sentence from the article.

*"Not only do they make pretty rings and necklaces, they are also very important to the nation's **economy**..."*

What does the word **economy** mean in this sentence?

A. Good use of natural resources

B. The way a system operates

C. Something that makes it possible to save or spend less money

D. The process by which goods and services are produced and sold

USING COMMAS IN COMPOUND SENTENCES

Commas join words, phrases, or two sentences to make a compound sentence. A comma goes between the first sentence and the coordinating conjunction. Coordinating conjunctions such as **and, but, for, or, nor, so**, and **yet** are connecting words.

> Example:
>
> The crystals on the bracelet look like diamonds. You cannot really tell the difference.
>
> The crystals on the bracelet look like diamonds, <u>so</u> you cannot really tell the difference.

Activity 1

Revise the compound sentences below. Insert a comma and coordinating conjunction, if needed. If the sentence is correct, write CORRECT.

1. Alexandria loved the diamond ring she bought it. _____

2. Wyatt wrote a report on diamond rain he included information that he learned in science class. _____

3. Jupiter is producing diamonds scientists cannot reach them. _____

4. Maria does not like the diamond necklace, yet she refuses to return it. _____

5. You can choose to study Jupiter you can choose to study Saturn. _____

Activity 2

Write four compound sentences using coordinating conjunctions of your choice. Be sure to use commas.

1. _____

2. _____

3. _____

4. _____

Solar Roadways

1 Can you imagine the snow melting right before your eyes while playing at the park on a cold winter day? Julie and Scott Brusaw have been working on an invention that would allow that to happen and more. Solar roadways are a new paving system that would improve and change the world as we know it. This new paving system can be placed on roads, highways, and driveways, and nearly anywhere under the sun. Solar panels made of glass would collect energy from the sun that can melt snow, stop power outages, and cut greenhouse gas pollution by nearly 75 percent.

Safer Roads for Drivers

2 Solar roadways would make the roads less dangerous for drivers. The solar panels would contain a heating element in the surface to prevent snow and ice from building up on the roads. Imagine having a solar driveway that never has to be shoveled to remove the snow! In addition, **LED lights** would be painted on the road to reduce vehicle accidents by seventy percent. The lights would allow drivers to see better at night and provide a warning when deer or other wild animals were entering the road.

Benefits to Home and Business Owners

3 Solar roadways carry power, along with **data signals**, to every home and business that is connected to the grid. Therefore, businesses and homeowners would receive electricity for telephones, cable TV, and even the Internet from the power grid that runs off of the sun's energy. Power shortages and outages would never be a problem again. People would no longer need to burn coal that causes pollution.

Are Solar Roadways Good for the Environment?

4 These new roadways can help clean up the environment by producing pure energy from the sun and decreasing pollution. Electric roads would make electric vehicles (EV) that run on batteries more **user-friendly**. EV owners could recharge their batteries in parking lots or rest stops. People could travel the same distance as with a gasoline-powered vehicle that creates carbon dioxide (CO_2), which pollutes the air. More people would be driving EVs, decreasing harmful greenhouse gases that pollute the environment.

Assistance for Developing Nations

5   In many areas of the world, getting clean drinking and bathing water is a challenge. Solar panels can provide needed power to create clean drinking water in **developing nations**. In addition, energy connections are not easily available for schools. The solar panels can help to provide education for children by producing energy that powers both lights and computers.

glossary

data signals: An indicator, such as a colored light, that serves as a means of communication.

LED lights: LEDs are small light bulbs that fit into tiny circuits. LED lighting can be more effective, longer lasting, and has a variety of uses.

FINDING MAIN IDEAS AND DETAILS

Use "Solar Roadways" to answer the following questions.

1. What is the **main idea** of the article?

_____

_____

2. List **three key details** to support the main idea of the article.

_____

_____

_____

3. Write a **summary** of the article.

_____

_____

_____

_____

DESCRIBING SCIENTIFIC CONCEPTS

Using "Solar Roadways," complete the chart below by writing either the feature or effect of each solar roadway item.

FEATURE	EFFECT
	Prevent snow and ice buildup
LED lights	
	Create clean drinking water in developing nations
	Carry electricity to business and homeowner
Solar panels	

UNDERSTANDING TEXT STRUCTURE

Use "Solar Roadways" to answer the following questions.

1. How is the paragraph under the subheading "Assistance for Developing Nations" **mainly structured**?

   A. problem and solution

   B. chronological order

   C. compare and contrast

   D. question and answer

2. Read the sentences below from the article.

   "Electric roads would make electric vehicles (EV) that run on batteries more user-friendly. EV owners could recharge their batteries in parking lots or rest stops."

   Which statement best describes the relationship between these sentences?

   A. The sentences make a comparison.

   B. The sentences describe two steps in a process.

   C. The first sentence explains the reason for the second.

   D. The first sentence gives the cause of the second sentence.

VOCABULARY DEVELOPMENT AND USE

After reading "Solar Roadways," look for words and phrases that you may not know. Identify clues to help you determine their meaning. Answer the questions below.

1. Read this sentence from the article.

    *"Electric roads would make electric vehicles (EV) that run on batteries more **user-friendly**."*

    What is the meaning of the phrase **user-friendly** in the sentence above?

    A. Easy to use
    B. Uses less energy
    C. Easy to understand
    D. Safer for the environment

2. Read this sentence from the article.

    *"Solar panels can provide needed power to create clean drinking water in **developing nations**."*

    What is the meaning of the phrase **developing nations**?

    A. Countries that are well developed
    B. Countries that are underdeveloped
    C. Countries that already use solar energy
    D. Countries that need to provide education for the children

3. What clues in the article helped you figure out the meaning to the phrases **user-friendly** and **developing nations**?

    _____

    _____

    _____

    _____

    _____

USING SYNONYMS

Synonyms are words that have, or almost have, the same meaning as each other.

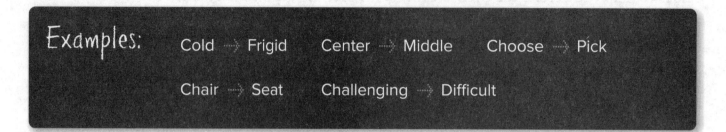

Examples: Cold ⇢ Frigid   Center ⇢ Middle   Choose ⇢ Pick

Chair ⇢ Seat   Challenging ⇢ Difficult

Match the words from the article on the left with their corresponding synonyms on the right.

Power	Advantage
Panel	Stop
Prevent	Lessen
Grid	Surroundings
Decrease	Network
Environment	Board
Benefit	Energy

CORRECTING SENTENCES

A complete sentence must express a complete thought and contain a subject and verb. A sentence fragment is missing the complete thought, the subject, or the verb. A run-on sentence is two or more complete thoughts joined together with incorrect punctuation.

Examples:

1. **Example of a fragment:** Solar roadways provide.

   This sentence fragment has a verb and subject but is missing a complete thought. To correct a sentence fragment, add a subject, a verb, and/or a complete thought.

   Corrected: Solar roadways provide energy from the sun.

2. **Example of a run-on sentence:** My mother has an electric vehicle, she doesn't know how to charge the batteries.

   Corrected: My mother has an electric vehicle, but she doesn't know how to charge the batteries.

   OR

   Corrected: My mother has an electric vehicle. She doesn't know how to charge the batteries.

Activity 1

Circle the sentence fragments. If a sentence is correct, write CORRECT next to it.

1. Solar roadways will improve the environment. _____

2. LED lights on highways. _____

3. Heating elements on the surface of roadways. _____

4. Power shortages will be a thing of the past. _____

Activity 2

Underline the run-on sentence.

1. Solar roadways can help developing nations children will have clean water to drink.

2. Electric vehicles decrease harmful greenhouse gases that pollute the environment.

Activity 3

Rewrite each sentence to correct each fragment or run-on sentence.

1. Solar roadways all over the city.

   _____.

2. Solar roadways can be placed.

   _____.

3. If we had a power outage.

   _____.

4. The lights went out we hid under the bed during the storm to stay warm.

   _____.

5. The solar panels melted the snow we didn't have to shovel the driveway.

   _____.

WRITE YOUR ESSAY

Put your thinking cap on! Use your imagination to create a new invention that will make a difference in people's lives! Write an essay about your invention and how and why it will help people.

Guidelines:

1. What do you want to invent? What help will it provide to people?

2. Develop at least three subtopics to support your main topic. A subtopic supports your main topic. Each one can be a subheading in your essay.

3. Perform research on the Internet or at your local library. Develop each subtopic with facts, concrete details, definitions, quotations from good sources, and any other related information that you may find. List your sources on a separate piece of paper.

4. Use linking words such as *another*, *for example*, *as*, *also*, *because*, *for*.

5. Provide a concluding paragraph to sum up the importance of your invention.

6. Use the graphic organizer to map out your story.

Topic Statement:

I want to invent a _____ because _____

_____

Your invention: What problem are you addressing? How will your invention make a difference and solve this problem? _____

_____

Subtopic 1: _____

_____

Subtopic 2: _____

_____

Subtopic 3: _____

_____

Remember to support each subtopic with facts, definitions, and any other

interesting information you find! _____

_____

Conclusion: _____

_____

_____

DEVELOP and CONCLUDE

Appreciate Our Land

Our planet is home to countless natural wonders. Almost anywhere you go on Earth, you can find beautiful places in nature. In the United States, many of these places are protected in national and state parks so that people from all over the world can visit and enjoy them. In this unit, you will learn about the history and beauty of two natural wonders, right here in our own country.

Hiking the Appalachian Trail

1 "It's a beautiful day. Let's go on a hike!" If you live close to the mountains or a forest, you may have heard those words before. Whether you are young or old, **hiking** can be a fun way to explore nature and get exercise. There are hiking trails all over the United States, but one of the longest and most famous is the **Appalachian Trail**, in the eastern part of the country. An estimated two to three million people visit and hike parts of the Appalachian Trail every year. Would you like to be one of them? Start your adventure by finding out more about hiking this **unique** trail!

A Very Long Walk

2 The Appalachian Trail is named after the Appalachian Mountains, a mountain range that stretches all the way from Georgia to Maine. The trail runs nearly the whole length of the mountain range, passing through parts of fourteen states. That means that from its beginning at Springer Mountain, Georgia to its end at Katahdin, Maine, the trail is about 2,180 miles long. Some experienced hikers travel the whole length of the trail, camping along the way. It can take anywhere from four to eight months to hike the Appalachian Trail that way. Not surprisingly, most people who visit the trail take much shorter day hikes!

Planning Your Hike

3 What is needed for a day hike on the Appalachian Trail? Hiking is fun, but it is also a difficult activity that can be dangerous if you do not prepare for it. First, you will need to find a responsible adult to go on your hike with you. Some hiking trails are very isolated, so it is best to hike in pairs or small groups. Second, you will need to pick a trail to hike. There are several things you should think about when picking your trail, such as length, difficulty, and location. If you are a beginning hiker, for example, you may want to choose a trail that is short, easy, and close to your home. Third, you will need to gather your equipment.

Hiking Equipment

4 For your hike, you will need to pack basic supplies and equipment. However, you do not want to pack so much that it will be too heavy for you to carry. One of the most important things to take with you is water. Hiking can be **strenuous** exercise, so it is important to stay well **hydrated**! You should also pack several small, lightweight snacks so that you do not run out of energy on the trail. The clothing you choose for hiking is another important part of your

equipment. It should be comfortable and easy to move around in. Because hiking is mainly walking and climbing, it is a good idea to wear **sturdy** shoes that will protect your feet, such as athletic shoes or boots. The weather and temperature sometimes change quickly, so it is also a good idea to bring a jacket. Other **essential** items to pack for your hike include a map or trail guide for the area where you are hiking, a **compass**, and a basic first aid kit.

Enjoying the Outdoors

5 On your hike, you will see beautiful scenery as well as many types of plants and animals. It is important to remember that for those living creatures, the land around the Appalachian Trail is home. As a visitor, you should be respectful of their home. Many parks, forests, and trails, including the Appalachian Trail, encourage hikers and other visitors to participate in "Leave No Trace" practices, such as making sure that no trash is left behind and leaving all plants and flowers in place instead of picking them. This helps keep the trail clean and beautiful so that future hikers can enjoy it just as much as you did.

6 In this article, you have learned some basic hiking tips for one of the longest continuous trails in the world. So next time someone says, "It's a beautiful day!" you can say, "Let's go for a hike on the Appalachian Trail!"

glossary

Appalachian Trail: A hiking trail extending through the Appalachian Mountains from central Maine to northern Georgia.

compass: An instrument for showing direction.

essential: Important.

experienced: Knowing a lot about something as a result of practice or experience.

hiking: Taking a long walk. Usually through the country or through rugged terrain, for enjoyment, exercise, or training.

hydrated: Having enough water in the body.

isolated: Away from other persons or things; remote.

strenuous: Requiring great effort, exertion, or hard work.

sturdy: Strong, hardy, or solid.

Digging Deeper

Find a Hike!

What if you don't live near the Appalachian Trail? No problem! There are thousands of hiking and walking trails all over the United States. No matter whether you live in a big city, a small town, or out in the country, there is probably a trail nearby.

FINDING MAIN IDEAS AND DETAILS

Use "Hiking the Appalachian Trail" to answer the following questions.

1. What is the **main idea** of the article?
   A. The Appalachian Trail is a famous trail where hikers of all experience levels can enjoy nature.
   B. Hikers on the Appalachian Trail should make sure that they wear comfortable clothing and shoes.
   C. The Appalachian Trail is 2,180 miles long and stretches from Georgia to Maine.
   D. Hikers can protect nature by making sure they do not leave any trash on the Appalachian Trail.

2. Write a **summary** of the article. Be sure to state the main idea with its supporting details in your own words. If you use information directly from the article, remember to use quotation marks.

   _____

   _____

EXPLAINING DETAILS

1. According to the article, why should hikers be careful to make sure they do not leave any trash behind or remove any plants from the trail? _____

   _____

2. Why is it important to prepare properly for a hiking trip?
   A. Most hiking trips take four to eight months, so hikers need large amounts of equipment and supplies.
   B. Unprepared hikers are more likely to hurt nature because they do not understand "Leave No Trace" practices.
   C. Hiking is a difficult physical activity that can be dangerous if people do not have the right equipment.
   D. Careful planning can prevent trails from becoming crowded by the two to three million people who hike every year.

Reading and Writing: Informational Texts

UNDERSTANDING TEXT STRUCTURE

Use "Hiking the Appalachian Trail" to answer the following questions.

Articles may contain more than one type of structure, such as chronological order, cause and effect, or problem and solution.

1. How is the article "Hiking the Appalachian Trail" **mainly structured**?

    A. problem and solution

    B. chronological order

    C. topics and subtopics

    D. cause and effect

2. Read the following sentences.

    "One of the most important things to take with you is water."
    *"Hiking can be **strenuous** exercise, so it is important to stay well **hydrated**!"*

    Which statement describes the relationship between these two sentences?

    A. The sentences make a comparison.

    B. The sentences describe two steps in a process.

    C. The second sentence is an effect of the first sentence.

    D. The second sentence is a cause of the first sentence.

3. How is the text structured in the section "Planning Your Hike?"

    A. problem and solution

    B. chronological order

    C. topics and subtopics

    D. cause and effect

4. Which text structure does the following sentence use? *"The weather and temperature sometimes change quickly, so it is also a good idea to bring a jacket."*

    A. problem and solution

    B. chronological order

    C. topics and subtopics

    D. cause and effect

EXPLAINING REASONS AND EVIDENCE

Every author has a purpose for writing. The author may write to present information to encourage the reader to believe something. The author will include reasons and evidence to support his or her points and influence readers to believe what is stated in the text.

Use the box below to write four pieces of evidence from the text that the author gives to support the claim that people need specific equipment and supplies for hiking.

Claim: "For your hike, you will need to pack basic supplies and equipment."

Evidence 1:

Evidence 2:

Evidence 3:

Evidence 4:

UNDERSTANDING ROOT WORDS

A *root* is a main word part that can be added to other word parts, such as suffixes and prefixes, to form words with common meanings. For example, the root *meter* means to measure.

Example: **Root:** meter **Origin:** Greek **Meaning:** measure

Word 1: therm**ometer** measures temperature

Word 2: od**ometer** measures miles driven in a vehicle

Circle the root in each bold word. From the box below, choose a root definition to match the sentence. Write its associated letter on the line provided.

1. The hiking trail went through rough **terrain**. _____

2. **Hydration** is very important for hikers. _____

3. He used a **pedometer** to measure how many steps he took on his hike. _____

4. The hiker put a **description** of the plants she saw in her journal. _____

Root Definitions

A. earth

B. write

C. water

D. foot

USING ANTONYMS

Antonyms are words that have opposite meanings.

Examples: good ⇢ bad   wet ⇢ dry   clean ⇢ dirty

Answer the following questions about antonyms.

1. Which of the following is an antonym for the word **unique** in paragraph 1?

    A. different   B. common   C. difficult   D. boring

2. Read this sentence from the article.

    *"Third, you will need to **gather** your equipment."*

    Which of the following is an antonym for the word **gather** in the sentence above?

    A. collect   B. move   C. gather   D. scatter

3. Read this sentence from the article.

    *"Because hiking is mainly walking and climbing, it is a good idea to wear **sturdy** shoes that will protect your feet, such as athletic shoes or boots."*

    Which of the following is an antonym for the word **sturdy** in the sentence above?

    A. normal   B. powerful   C. delicate   D. waterproof

4. Read this sentence from the article.

    *"Other **essential** items to pack for your hike include a map or trail guide for the area where you are hiking, a compass, and a basic first aid kit."*

    Which of the following is an antonym for the word **essential** in the sentence above?

    A. unimportant   B. necessary   C. easy   D. interesting

WRITE YOUR OPINION

After reading the article, do you think you would enjoy hiking the Appalachian Trail? Write an opinion essay stating your answer. Be sure your essay has a topic sentence, or main idea, that tells your opinion. Use information from the text to support your opinion. Next, list three reasons why you believe you would or would not enjoy hiking the Appalachian Trail. Finally, write a conclusion that restates your opinion. Use the graphic organizer below to help you plan your essay.

Introduction (Create a topic sentence): _____

_____

_____

Body (Describe three reasons for your opinion): _____

_____

_____

_____

_____

_____

_____

Conclusion (Restate opinion): _____

_____

_____

_____

_____

The Grand Canyon

1 Have you ever stood next to something really big? Maybe it was a very tall building or a large tree. Did you feel very small by comparison? That is how some people feel when they see the Grand Canyon for the first time. Much bigger than any building or tree, the Grand Canyon is one of the most famous natural wonders of the United States. Every year, between four and five million people from all over the world travel to the state of Arizona to see this amazing sight.

What is the Grand Canyon?

2 A **canyon** is a deep valley with very steep sides. The Grand Canyon was carved into the land over millions of years by the Colorado River, which still flows through the bottom of the canyon today. As the water moved over the landscape, it carried away layer after layer of rock and dirt through a process called erosion. So much **erosion** has occurred at the Grand Canyon that many different layers of rock can be seen in the canyon walls. Some of the layers of rock are over a billion years old! Normally, they would be buried deep in the ground, but the unique erosion at the canyon has made them visible. Today, **geologists** and other scientists study these rock layers to find out what the earth was like hundreds of millions of years ago.

Life In the Grand Canyon

3 The Grand Canyon is more than just rocks and a river; it is also home to thousands of **diverse** species of plants and animals! Scientists have identified at least 1,750 types of plants that grow in and around the Grand Canyon. There are also 373 species of birds, ninety-two species of mammals, fifty-seven species of reptiles and amphibians, and eighteen species of fish. At least twenty of the animal species that live in the Grand Canyon are **endemic** to the area and are found nowhere else in the world. In order for these species to survive, the Grand Canyon must be protected.

Protecting the Grand Canyon

4 Many years ago, people realized what a unique place the Grand Canyon is and decided that it should be protected. Therefore, in 1919, the United States government declared the Grand Canyon a national park. National parks (like Grand Canyon National Park) are areas where the land is set aside for **conservation** so that people now and in the future can enjoy natural scenery. Even though the Grand Canyon is protected by the government, it takes **cooperation**

from everyone to keep it clean and beautiful. Park rangers, scientists, and others work hard to educate visitors about how they can "leave no trace," that is, enjoy the park but disturb nature as little as possible.

Visiting the Grand Canyon

5 Does "leaving no trace" at the Grand Canyon mean that you cannot do anything but look at it? Of course not! There are lots of ways that visitors can enjoy the Grand Canyon. Inside Grand Canyon National Park, roads and trails lead visitors to many lookout points where they can see beautiful views of the canyon. There are also education centers and museums, where visitors can learn about the history and the science of the Grand Canyon. Travelers who enjoy hiking and camping can choose from many trails and campsites both at the top and the bottom of the canyon. Some people even take mule rides into the canyon or float down the Colorado River inside the canyon on a raft!

6   From its unique plants and animals to its beautiful rock layers, the Grand Canyon is truly a special place. Millions of people around the world have already been able to enjoy this **magnificent** natural wonder. With proper care and protection, the Grand Canyon can be preserved and shared with millions more.

glossary

canyon: A deep valley with steep sides.

conservation: The protection of natural lands and resources from loss, pollution, or waste.

cooperation: The act of working together.

diverse: Showing a great deal of variety; very different.

endemic: Something that is found in only a single region and nowhere else in the world.

erosion: Wearing away of the earth's surface by wind or water.

geologist: A scientist who studies what the earth is made of and how it formed, often through the study of rocks.

FINDING MAIN IDEAS AND DETAILS

Use "The Grand Canyon" to answer the following questions.

1. What is another good title for the article?

    A. Wildlife of the Grand Canyon

    B. Grand Canyon in Danger!

    C. The Grand Canyon: A Natural Wonder

    D. The History of the Grand Canyon

2. Which sentence is **least** important to include in a summary?

   A. The Grand Canyon was carved into the land over millions of years by the Colorado River, which still flows through the bottom of the canyon today.

   B. Some people take mule rides into the canyon or float down the Colorado River inside the canyon on a raft.

   C. The Grand Canyon is home to thousands of diverse species of plants and animals, including twenty endemic species.

   D. Even though the Grand Canyon is protected by the government, it takes cooperation from everyone to keep it clean and beautiful.

3. Write a **summary** of the article. Remember to state the main idea and the most important supporting details of the main idea.

   _____

   _____

   _____

   _____

EXPLAINING RELATIONSHIPS

Use "The Grand Canyon" to answer the following questions.

1. List at least **three ways** that visitors can enjoy the Grand Canyon. Use details from the article to answer the question.

   _____

   _____

   _____

2. Explain how the Grand Canyon was formed, using details from the article.

   _____

   _____

   _____

Reading and Writing: Informational Texts

UNDERSTANDING TEXT STRUCTURE

Use "The Grand Canyon" to answer the following questions.

1. How is the text **mainly structured**?

    A. topics and subtopics

    B. problem and solution

    C. chronological order

    D. cause and effect

2. Read the following sentences:

    "Many years ago, people realized what a unique place the Grand Canyon is and decided that it should be protected. Therefore, in 1919, the United States government declared the Grand Canyon a national park."

    Which statement best describes the relationship between the two sentences?

    A. The two sentences compare similar events.

    B. The two sentences contrast differing viewpoints.

    C. The second sentence explains the first sentence.

    D. The second sentence is an effect of the first sentence.

IDENTIFYING REASONS AND EVIDENCE

Every author has a purpose for writing an article. Authors include reasons and evidence to support their point of view. Use the boxes below to write two pieces of evidence from the text that the author uses to support the point that the Grand Canyon is a natural wonder that should be protected.

Evidence 1:

Evidence 2:

EXPLAINING DATA

You can use information presented in charts to understand what you read.

After reading "The Grand Canyon," use the chart to answer the questions below.

Measuring the Grand Canyon

The estimated volume of the Grand Canyon, or how much space is inside it, is 4.17 trillion cubic meters. That means that to fill up all the space in the Grand Canyon with water, you would need enough water for almost 1.67 billion Olympic-size swimming pools!

...Did you know?

From its start in the Rocky Mountains of Colorado to its end at the Gulf of California in Mexico, the Colorado River is 1,450 miles long!

Length: 277 miles of the Colorado River (includes bends in the river)

Average depth from rim to canyon bottom: 1 mile (5,280 feet)

Average width from the North Rim to the South Rim: 10 miles

Maximum width between rims: 18 miles

Minimum width between rims: 600 feet

1. How many miles of the Colorado River flow through the Grand Canyon? _____

2. What is the average distance from the top of the canyon to the bottom?

    A. 600 feet   B. 10 miles   C. 5,280 feet   D. 18 miles

3. How wide is the Grand Canyon at its widest point?

    A. 277 miles   B. 18 miles   C. 10 miles   D. 1 mile

4. Is there any place where the Grand Canyon is deeper than it is wide? Explain your answer.

_____

_____

USING REFERENCE MATERIALS

Use "The Grand Canyon" to answer the following questions.

1. Read this sentence from the article.

   *"As the water moved over the landscape, it carried away layer after layer of rock and dirt through a process called **erosion**."*

   Look below at the dictionary entry of erosion. What part of speech is erosion as used in the article? _____ .

   Noun: /əˈrōZHən/

   : wearing away of the earth's surface by wind or water

2. Underline the dictionary entry that contains the correct definition for the word "endemic" in paragraph 3.

   Adjective: /enˈdemik/

   A. : (of a disease or condition) regularly found among particular people or in a certain area.

   B. : (of a plant or animal) native or restricted to a certain country or area.

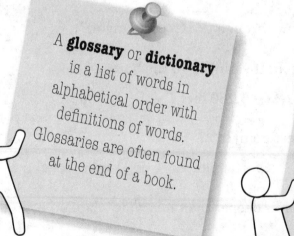

A **glossary** or **dictionary** is a list of words in alphabetical order with definitions of words. Glossaries are often found at the end of a book.

The dictionary is your best reading tool! It helps you understand what a word means and how it should be used.

SYNONYMS

Synonyms are words that have the same, or almost the same, meaning.

Practice using synonyms and answer the questions below.

1. Read this sentence from the article.

    *"Millions of people around the world have already been able to enjoy this **magnificent** natural wonder."*

    Which word is a synonym for **magnificent**?

    A. spectacular   B. enormous   C. unique   D. pretty

2. Which word is a synonym for **cooperation** as used in paragraph 4 of the article?

    A. effort   B. education   C. idea   D. teamwork

WRITE YOUR OPINION

Do you believe that natural areas like the Grand Canyon should be protected by the government? Write an opinion essay stating your answer. Be sure your essay has a topic sentence, or main idea, that tells your opinion. Use evidence from the text to support your claim. Next, list three reasons why you believe or do not believe that natural areas should be protected. Finally, write a conclusion that restates your opinion. Use the graphic organizer below to help you plan your essay.

Introduction (Create a topic sentence): _____

_____

_____

_____

Body (Describe three reasons for your opinion): _____

_____

_____

_____

_____

_____

_____

_____

Conclusion (Restate opinion): _____

_____

_____

_____

_____

In the Wild

The Endangered Species Act of 1973 (ESA) provides for the protection of animals that are endangered or threatened and the areas in which these animals live. The ESA also has guidelines that limit the hunting and transporting of these animals. We are responsible for making sure that this world remains a happy home for all of the creatures that live in it and to do what we can to save those that may be in danger of survival.

The Bald Eagle: An Endangered Species Success Story

1   Which is the most famous bird in the United States? The bald eagle, of course! A national symbol since 1782, this beautiful creature—with its striking white head and tail feathers—is easy to recognize. Even with all its fame, however, the bald eagle nearly became extinct, or died out completely, 50 years ago. Luckily, the U.S. government passed many laws just in time to save this beautiful bird.

2   To understand why the bald eagle almost became extinct, it is important to know how the bird lives. Bald eagles usually live close to water because they mostly eat fish. They use large trees to build their nests, which can be as wide as 10 feet (3.1 m), and can weigh 1,000 pounds or more! Eagles mate for life, and females lay two to three eggs a year. Like all wildlife, their natural habitat is important to their survival.

3   In the 1780s, about 100,000 nesting bald eagles lived in America. A century later, the bald eagle's population was much smaller. How did this happen? One reason was as the United States grew, people cut the bald eagle's trees for lumber or construction. People shot these birds for sport or to protect their livestock. By 1940, the government realized the bald eagle was in danger. It passed what is now called the Bald and Golden Eagle Protection Act to keep people from harming these birds.

4   Still, the bald eagle was in trouble. By 1963, there were only 487 nesting pairs left in the continental United States. What was going wrong? The biggest problem was the use of DDT, a chemical introduced in the 1940s to kill harmful insects. When it was sprayed near water, DDT was also absorbed by fish that the bald eagles would eat. The DDT caused female eagles to lay eggs with very thin shells that broke easily. As a result, very few eaglets, or baby eagles, were being born. Then, in 1972, the U.S. Environmental Protection Agency banned, or stopped, the use of DDT. This was great news for the bald eagle!

5   Other laws helped too. In 1967, the Endangered Species Act was passed to protect the bald eagle and other animals that were close to extinction. The Migratory Bird Treaty Act passed in 1972, which also protected the bald eagle when it flew to other countries such as Mexico. By 2006, nearly 10,000 pairs of bald eagles were nesting in America. In 2007, its population increased by so much, the bird was taken off the endangered list. The bald eagle is a true endangered species success story.

FINDING MAIN IDEAS AND DETAILS

Use "The Bald Eagle: An Endangered Species Success Story" to answer the following questions.

1. What is the **main idea** of the article?

    A. The bald eagle nearly became extinct, but it is now increasing in numbers because of U.S. government protection.

    B. The bald eagle has been the national symbol of the United States since 1782, and it needs to be protected from extinction.

    C. The bald eagle almost became extinct from a dangerous chemical that was banned in 1972 by the U.S. government.

    D. The bald eagle decreased in numbers to near extinction because people in the United States destroyed its natural habitat.

2. Which **key detail** from the article supports the main idea?

    A. "In the 1780s, about 100,000 nesting bald eagles lived in America."

    B. "Bald eagles usually live close to water because they mostly eat fish."

    C. "By 2006, nearly 10,000 pairs of bald eagles were nesting in America."

    D. "The bald eagle is a true endangered species success story."

EXPLAINING IDEAS AND EVENTS

Identify the important ideas from the text. Answer the questions below.

1. Why did the U.S. Environmental Protection Agency ban DDT?

    A. The EPA wanted bald eagles to safely fly to other countries.

    B. DDT caused bald eagles to lay eggs with thin shells that broke easily.

    C. The EPA wanted to stop people from killing bald eagles.

    D. DDT killed harmful insects that bald eagles would eat.

2. Why is the bald eagle so famous in the United States?

    A. It has been a national symbol for the United States since 1782.

    B. It builds nests all over the United States that weigh 1,000 pounds.

    C. It lives in tall treetops and lays two to three eggs every year in the United States.

    D. It has been on the endangered species list in the United States since 1967.

UNDERSTANDING TEXT STRUCTURE

Use "The Bald Eagle: An Endangered Species Success Story" to answer the following questions.

Chronology tells the events in the order they happened. Problem/ solution presents a problem and then discusses its solution

1. What is the overall structure of paragraphs 3 and 4? How would the article read if these paragraphs were switched? Explain.

_____

_____

_____

_____

2. How does the information in paragraph 2 relate to information in paragraphs 3 and 4? Explain.

_____

_____

_____

_____

3. How would the article change if paragraph 5 became paragraph 2 instead? Explain.

_____

_____

_____

_____

USING CHARTS TO GATHER INFORMATION

Using "The Bald Eagle: An Endangered Species Success Story," study the following chart to understand more about the bald eagle. Complete the activity.

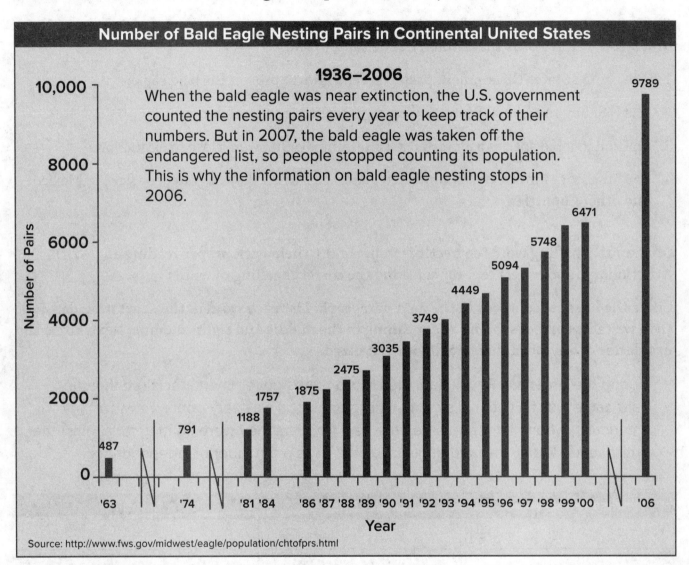

Number of Bald Eagle Nesting Pairs in Continental United States

1936–2006

When the bald eagle was near extinction, the U.S. government counted the nesting pairs every year to keep track of their numbers. But in 2007, the bald eagle was taken off the endangered list, so people stopped counting its population. This is why the information on bald eagle nesting stops in 2006.

Source: http://www.fws.gov/midwest/eagle/population/chtofprs.html

Look at the bar chart above on bald eagle nesting pairs. What can you say about the bald eagle population between 1963 and 2006? Does the chart support the information in the article? Does it provide more information about bald eagle nesting pairs? Explain.

_____

_____

_____

MASTERING CAPITALIZATION

Capitalizing proper nouns helps the reader know which words are the names of people as well as certain important places and special things.

Circle the words that should be capitalized in the following sentences. Put a line through the first letter of the words that should not be capitalized.

1. The United States Government passed several laws to protect the bald eagle.

2. The U.S. Environmental Protection agency stopped the use of ddt.

3. The endangered species act created a list of Animals that were close to extinction.

4. The migratory bird treaty act protected bald eagles when they migrated, or flew, to Mexico and other Countries.

Challenge: Spelling words correctly is important to help with proper reading and writing. A dictionary is your best tool for checking the correct spelling of words.

Circle the misspelled words in the next paragraph. List each word in the chart provided and then write its correct spelling and meaning in the middle and right columns. Next, circle the first letter of any word that should be capitalized.

During the American Revulution, the United States government declaired that the bald eagle was its national symbol. This glorius bird was very populore with many americans, who felt it represented the very freedom they were fighting for against the british. even today, the bald eagle is looked to as a reminder of independance.

	Misspelled Word	Correct Spelling	Meaning
1.			
2.			
3.			
4.			
5.			
6.			

The Plan for the Bald Eagle

A reporter from a radio show on wildlife is interviewing an employee from the U.S. Fish & Wildlife Service (FWS) about a program that studies the bald eagle population in the continental United States.

1 **Reporter:** We are very happy to have you on our show today!

2 **FWS employee:** Thank you for this opportunity to talk about the Post-delisting Monitoring Program for the bald eagle.

3 **Reporter:** What does "post-delisting" mean?

4 **FWS employee:** As you know, "post" means after and "delist" means to be taken off a list. Basically, we are studying the bald eagle population after it has been taken off the U.S. government's endangered list of animals. We are now monitoring, or watching, the bald eagle to make sure this species of bird does not come close to extinction again.

5 **Reporter:** Could you please give us a brief history about that?

6 **FWS employee:** Fifty years ago, the bald eagle was nearly extinct. There were slightly over 400 nesting pairs in the country. Then in 1967, the Endangered Species Act was passed. The bald eagle was immediately put on the government's list of endangered animals. For several reasons, the bald eagle nesting pair population increased to nearly 10,000 within forty years. In 2007, it was officially delisted.

7 **Reporter:** Does this mean that the bald eagle is no longer protected from being killed or harmed by people?

8 **FWS employee:** No, the bald eagle is still protected by the U.S. government through the Bald and Golden Eagle Protection Act and the Migratory Bird Treaty Act. The Post-delisting Monitoring Plan, or "the plan" as we call it, has been designed to make sure the bald eagle does not get close to extinction again.

9 **Reporter:** How does the plan work?

10 **FWS employee:** The plan began in 2009 and is designed to last twenty years. Every five years, certain bald eagle nests are checked in eagle habitats across the continental United States. Occupied nests get compared to the number of new nests that are found in the same area. The FWS works with all forty-eight states in this effort.

11 **Reporter:** What happens if you find the bald eagle population decreases in twenty years?

12 **FWS employee:** If the numbers decrease, we find out what is causing the drop in population and try to fix the problem. We would also have the bald eagle listed as "endangered" again to make sure it has even more protection from the U.S. government.

13 **Reporter:** This sounds like a great plan! Thank you again for speaking on our show.

14 **FWS employee:** Thank you!

COMPARE AND CONTRAST ARTICLES

After reading "The Bald Eagle: An Endangered Species Success Story" and "The Plan for the Bald Eagle," evaluate the different ways the information is presented. Then, fill in the charts below.

1. In this first section, you are going to evaluate how the first- and second-hand accounts on the same topic are **similar**.

"The Bald Eagle: An Endangered Species Success Story"	"The Plan for the Bald Eagle"

2. In this next section, you are going to evaluate how the first- and second-hand accounts on the same topic are **different**.

"The Bald Eagle: An Endangered Species Success Story"	"The Plan for the Bald Eagle"

COMBINING INFORMATION FROM TWO TEXTS

Reread "The Bald Eagle: An Endangered Species Success Story" and "The Plan for the Bald Eagle." Write a paragraph with a main idea about eagles in which you combine information from both sources. Remember to say what source your information came from. Use phrases such as "According to," and "As discussed in."

Main topic or idea:

_____

_____

_____

_____

_____

_____

_____

_____

_____

_____

_____

_____

_____

_____

_____

_____

_____

WRITE YOUR EXPLANATION

As you have read in the "Bald Eagle: An Endangered Species Success Story," the bald eagle's tale is an amazing one! Today, this bird is no longer facing extinction, but many other animals are.

Write an essay about an endangered animal. What animal will you choose? Where does it live and how does it survive? Why is it extinct or close to extinction? What is being done to help? Most importantly, what evidence from the two texts in this unit can you relate to the endangered animal that you chose to write about?

Use the graphic organizer to gather your facts. Then write your essay starting with an interesting introduction that includes your main idea, a discussion of your facts, and a strong conclusion that summarizes your ideas. Remember to say where you found the facts included in your essay.

The _____ I chose to write about is _____.
Fact 1:
Fact 2:
Fact 3:
Fact 4:
Fact 5:

Introduction (Include your main idea): _____

_____

_____

_____

First paragraph (Use supporting detail): _____

_____

_____

_____

Second paragraph (Use supporting detail): _____

_____

_____

_____

Third paragraph (Use supporting detail): _____

_____

_____

_____

Conclusion (Summarize your ideas): _____

_____

_____

_____

Fishzilla: The Snakehead Fish

1   Can you imagine a fish that can live out of water for several days? A fish that many say will eat anything in its path? A fish that some claim can walk across land? Sounds like a creature from the latest monster movie, but is it?

2   Do not be **alarmed**, but unfortunately, the snakehead fish—nicknamed Frankenfish and Fishzilla—is very real. Native to parts of Asia, this fish is considered an **invasive** species in America. This means it has no natural predators that would kill it in the wild. As a result, snakeheads have the ability to destroy all **aquatic** life and damage a complete **ecosystem**.

3   Named for the snakelike scales that cover its head, this freshwater fish has a mouth full of sharp teeth to feed its hungry appetite. Its slimy body can grow to be 4 feet (1.2 meters) long. Snakeheads mate several times a year, and females can lay tens of thousands of eggs at one time. The snakehead can breathe air from a special sac in its body, so it is able to live out of water for three to four days.

4   Many government websites claim a young snakehead can "walk" across land by **wriggling** its body to and fro until it reaches water. One source states this is not true of the northern snakehead, the most common species of the four types of snakeheads found, so far, in America. Whether snakeheads can walk or not, they have spread to several states across the country.

5   How did they get here? Until recently, people could buy live snakeheads from pet stores and fresh fish markets in many states. Some of these people would **release** the fish into freshwater because it had grown too big for their fish tanks. Others freed the snakehead as part of a religious ceremony. Because of these **careless actions**, the snakehead problem may now be out of control.

6   Wildlife officials have tried to stop the snakehead. When snakeheads were found in a Maryland pond, a chemical was used to kill them, but it destroyed the other fish too. The officials thought this would stop the problem, but they were wrong. Two years later, snakeheads were discovered in the 380-mile Potomac River. Because wildlife officials could not poison the whole river, they tried different ways to kill this fish, with little success.

7   There is a new way of decreasing the snakehead population, however—eating them! People say their meat is delicious. So far, fishermen have caught and sold 8,000 pounds of snakeheads each year in the Potomac River since 2012. This seems to be the best way to fight this invasive fish.

FINDING MAIN IDEAS AND DETAILS

Use "Fishzilla: The Snakehead Fish" to answer the following questions.

1. What is the **main idea** of the article?

   A. Snakeheads are unusual fish because their heads have snakelike scales.

   B. Snakeheads can damage an ecosystem because they have very sharp teeth.

   C. Snakeheads are causing problems in America because they have no natural enemies.

   D. Snakeheads are the most unusual fish in an ecosystem because they can breathe air.

2. Read this sentence from the article.

   "Whether snakeheads can walk or not, they have spread to several states across the country."

   Which **key detail** supports the main idea of this sentence?

   A. "Fishermen have caught and sold, 8,000 pounds of snakeheads each year."

   B. "Two years later, snakeheads were discovered in the 380-mile Potomac River."

   C. "When snakeheads were found in a Maryland pond, a chemical was used to kill them, but it destroyed the other fish too."

   D. "Until recently, people could buy live snakeheads from pet stores and fresh fish markets in many states."

EXPLAINING IDEAS AND EVENTS

Using "Fishzilla: The Snakehead Fish," connect the information in the text to explain why specific events happen.

1. Match the **cause** with its direct **effect**:

   1. poisoning a pond
   2. mating several times a year
   3. releasing snakeheads into water
   4. eating snakeheads

   a. ecosystems are in danger
   b. population decreases
   c. all wildlife dies
   d. tens of thousands of eggs are laid

2. Why can a snakehead live out of water for several days?

   A. It has a special sac that lets it breathe air.

   B. It uses its body to travel across land.

   C. It can eat anything that is in its path.

   D. It has no natural enemies to stop it.

EXPLAINING REASONS AND EVIDENCE

After reading the following sentence from the article, answer the questions below using information from the text in your responses.

   *"Because of these **careless actions**, the snakehead problem may now be out of control."*

1. What does the writer mean by **careless actions**? Provide examples from the text to support this point. Do you agree that these actions are careless? Why or why not?

   _____

   _____

2. What evidence can you find in the article that supports the writer's point that "the snakehead problem may now be out of control?" Do you agree with the author? Why or why not? Use evidence from the text.

   _____

   _____

   _____

UNDERSTANDING THE CLUES

Use "Fishzilla: The Snakehead Fish" to answer the following questions.

1. *"Some of these people would **release** the fish into freshwater because it had grown too big for their fish tanks."*

   What does **release** mean?

   A. to carry

   B. to lift up

   C. to grasp

   D. to set free

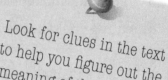

Look for clues in the text to help you figure out the meaning of the words in this lesson.

2. *"Do not be **alarmed**, but unfortunately, the snakehead fish— nicknamed Frankenfish and Fishzilla—is very real."*

   What does the word **alarmed** mean?

   A. to wake up

   B. to feel bad

   C. to be concerned

   D. to be mistaken

VOCABULARY DEVELOPMENT AND USE

Words that are specific to an area of study are called *domain specific*. *Domain* means "area," and *specific* means "particular." Answer the questions below.

Read the sentence from the article:

"As a result, snakeheads have the ability to destroy all **aquatic** *life and damage a complete ecosystem."*

When you read a new word, does it sometimes remind you of a similar word? For example, can you think of a word that is similar to *aquatic*?

aquatic   is similar to   aquarium

1. Where does a snakehead live? _____

    What lives in an aquarium? _____

2. Now put the information together! What do you think **aquatic** means? Explain.

    _____

3. Use the word **aquatic** in a sentence.

    _____

4. What does the word **system** mean?

    _____

5. The word part *eco-* means "habitat" or "environment." Now put the information together! What do you think **ecosystem** means? _____

    _____

6. Use the word **ecosystem** in a sentence.

    _____

USING REFERENCE MATERIALS

Read the following sentence from the article. Then read the dictionary entry. Answer the questions that follow.

"Native to parts of Asia, this fish is considered an **invasive** *species in America."*

> Invasive
>
> Adjective: /in·va·sive/
>
> 1. : tending to spread
>
> 2. : involving entry into the living body

1. Which dictionary entry provides the correct definition for the word **invasive** as used in the sentence above?

    A. 1

    B. 2

2. What part of speech is *invasive*? _____

3. How many syllables does the word *invasive* have? _____

4. If an invasive species has no natural predators, what must *predator* mean? *Clue: A predator can kill something.* _____

CHOOSING THE RIGHT WORDS

When you are writing, be sure to use words and phrases that say exactly what you mean. Read the following sentence from the text to answer the questions.

"Many government websites claim a young snakehead can 'walk' across land by **wriggling** *its body to and fro until it reaches water."*

What does the word **wriggling** mean? How would the meaning of the sentence change if the writer used the word "moving" instead? Which is the better word choice? Explain.

_____

_____

_____

REVIEW

Reading Fluency

Adults: Time your student reading aloud for one minute. Make a note of where your student is at the end of one minute. (Your student should be able to read 120–140 words per minute.) Count the total number of errors and subtract that from the number of words read. This will give you the total number of words read per minute. Then, have your student continue reading to the end of the article and answer the questions that follow.

A Grizzly Tale of Survival

Large, fast, and powerful—the grizzly bear has long been an image of the American West. 16
A subspecies of the brown bear, grizzly bears have a huge lump on their back that is all 34
muscle. This gives them extra strength to dig holes on the sides of hills to make dens to 52
hibernate (to rest or remain inactive) during the long winter months. 63

When standing on its hind feet, grizzly bears can be measured at 6–7 (1.5–2.5 meters) 78
feet tall! They can run up to 35 miles an hour in short spurts when chasing prey. But like 97
many wild animals in the United States, its population has decreased rapidly as more 111
humans have moved into the grizzly bear's natural **habitat**. 120

In the early 1800s, over 50,000 grizzly bears roamed across part of the West in 135
America. Forty years ago, a total of 1,500 grizzlies were believed to be alive. Then in 151
1975, the grizzly bear was listed as **threatened** by the Endangered Species Act. The 165
term "threatened" means that the population of a species has become so low that it is 181
close to being labeled as endangered, which means close to **extinction**. However, the 194
grizzly bear population is growing strong because of the protection it has received under 208
the Endangered Species Act (ESA). 213

Today, the bear can be found in five ecosystems across the Western states. Of these 228
ecosystems, growth of the grizzly bear population in 236
Yellowstone National Park has been remarkable. The 243
population increased from 136 in the mid-1970s to nearly 252
600 by 2007. This means that its **recovery**, the process in 263
which a threatened or endangered animal has been protected 272
from harm, has been successful. Because of this increase in 282
the grizzly bear population, the U.S. Fish and Wildlife Service 292

glossary

extinction: When a plant or animal species dies out completely

(FWS) had the grizzly bear **delisted** from the ESA in 2007. However, nature groups fought   306
to keep the bear protected, so the grizzly bear was again listed as threatened in 2009. In   323
January 2020, the FWS initiated a five-year status review of the grizzly bear.   337

Activity 1

Use "A Grizzly Tale of Survival" to answer the following questions.

1. Match each domain-specific word with its meaning.

   1. Ecosystem   a. no longer existing

   2. Endangered   b. everything that exists in a specific environment

   3. Extinction   c. no longer protected by the ESA

   4. Delisted   d. close to extinction

2. According to the ESA, what is the difference between **endangered** and **threatened**?

   _____

   _____

3. Write a sentence describing a wild animal's **habitat** that you have seen or have read about.

   _____

   _____

4. What does it mean to **delist** the grizzly bear from the Endangered Species Act? Explain.

   _____

   _____

5. Is the grizzly bear an **invasive** species to the American West? Explain.

   _____

   _____

Activity 2

Use the "In the Wild" articles to answer the following questions.

1. Write a glossary entry describing the bald eagle, grizzly bear, and snakehead fish.

    A. Bald eagle: _____

    B. Grizzly bear: _____

    C. Snakehead fish: _____

2. Match the word or phrase with a word that is similar but with a more specific meaning.

    1. hole   a. species

    2. group   b. argument

    3. walk   c. roam

    4. type of animal   d. den

    5. disagreement   e. population

Dictionaries, glossaries, and thesauruses are all excellent tools to help you learn the meaning of new words.

UNDERSTAND

Using "A Grizzly Tale of Survival," answer the following questions.

1. What is the **main idea** of "A Grizzly Tale of Survival"?

   _____

   _____

2. Provide **key details** from the article that support the main idea.

   _____

   _____

3. How is the word **recovery** used in this article?

   _____

   _____

4. What does **hibernate** mean?

   _____

   _____

5. What point did the writer make about the grizzly bear in the first sentence of the article? Provide evidence from the article to support your answer.

   _____

   _____

6. Provide evidence from the article that supports the writer's statement, "However, the grizzly bear population is growing strong because of the protection it has received under the Endangered Species Act (ESA)."

   _____

   _____

DISCOVER

Write Your Essay

The bald eagle and the grizzly bear are amazing success stories about how both species of animals survived extinction. Unfortunately, there are a number of animals that are now extinct. For this assignment, choose an animal to write about that is now extinct. Research the animal from books and the Internet.

Put your thinking cap on! Imagine that there are only a few more of these animals alive. You have been tasked with writing a newspaper article to inform an entire city of what must be done to save these animals. Quick, urgent action is needed! Write a clear topic and use facts, definitions, evidence, and examples from the articles in this unit to support your ideas.

Remember to link ideas together using words and phrases, such as "because" and "for example." Choose accurate and exact language and domain-specific words to present your ideas and key details. Write a strong conclusion that summarizes your information and calls to action the residents of your city to save the animals.

Introduction (Include main idea):

Topic idea (Supported by evidence):

Topic idea (Supported by evidence):

Topic idea (Supported by evidence):

Conclusion (Summarize ideas):

Reading and Writing: Literature

Short Fiction

Reading literature provides a look into an author's thoughts and feelings. It also reflects our world and the different ways that people behave. Even though the material in this section is fictional, valuable life lessons can be learned.

Writing about literature will cause you to organize your thoughts and to clearly state what you think and feel. As you write, new discoveries in your thinking will create connections to ideas and concepts that you already know. Working through what at first may seem challenging will only open new pathways of learning, understanding, and communicating.

In this section, you will read short stories, poems, myths, and fables with amazing plots, interesting characters, and beautiful word pictures.

Reading literature teaches you how other people behave together in the world, and writing about literature teaches you about yourself!

The word *fiction* is used to describe pieces of writing that tell a made-up story. The characters and events in fiction come from the imagination of the author. In this unit, you will practice reading, thinking, and writing about short stories.

Before we get into reading the stories, let's first talk about Rudyard Kipling, author of *The Jungle Book,* from which the short story "Rikki-Tikki-Tavi" is taken. His piece *The Jungle Book*, is a story about Mowgli, a young boy raised by a wolf, and inspired the beloved Disney movie that was made in 1967 carrying the same name. Born in 1865, Kipling was an English short-story writer, poet, and novelist. As one of the most popular writers in England, he became the first English-language and youngest writer to receive the Nobel Prize in Literature in 1907. Kipling's stories are classic, and he continues to be a celebrated writer of children's literature throughout the world.

Rikki-Tikki-Tavi

1   Some time ago in India there lived a young mongoose named Rikki-Tikki-Tavi. Now, a mongoose is a small animal with the fur of a cat, the face of a weasel, and a tail that fluffs up like a bottle-brush. As it runs through the grass, it makes the sound "Rikk-tikk-tikki-tikki-tchk!", and that is how this young mongoose got his name.

2   One day, Rikki-Tikki-Tavi was washed far away from his home by a flood. A little boy named Teddy found him and thought that he was dead.

3   "He's not dead," said Teddy's father. "Here. Let's dry him off."

4   When Rikki-Tikki woke up, the whole family was watching him. But because mongooses are very curious, and the family had saved him and given him food, he was not scared of them. Instead, he explored the house, and decided he liked it very much.

5   Teddy's mother was worried. "Don't you think that it will bite our son?" she asked her husband at bedtime when she saw Rikki-Tikki curled up on a pillow in Teddy's bed. "After all, it is a wild animal."

6   "Nonsense," said the father. "Our boy has never been safer. Mongooses can kill snakes, you know." Teddy's mother was terrified by the idea of a snake hurting her son, so Rikki-Tikki was allowed to stay.

7   The next day, he decided to go exploring again, this time in the gardens. There he met two birds, who were singing a very sad song. "What is wrong?" asked Rikki-Tikki. The male bird, Darzee, answered him. "We are sad because one of our babies fell from the nest and was eaten by Nag."

8   "That is very sad!" agreed Rikki-Tikki. Then he asked, "Who is Nag?"

9   Before Darzee or his wife could answer, a hissing sound came from the grass and suddenly the head of a large cobra appeared, its wide hood spread threateningly. "I am Nag. Look at me, and be afraid!" the cobra hissed. It lifted the front part of its body completely off the ground and swayed back and forth like a dandelion tuft in the wind, ready to strike at any moment.

10 Rikki-Tikki was only scared for a second before he remembered that he was a mongoose, and that even though he had never met a live cobra before, his mother had fed him plenty of dead ones, because the whole job of adult mongooses is to fight and eat snakes. He decided to meet Nag's challenge.

11 "So you are the great Nag," he replied. "What makes you think it is right to eat baby birds?"

12 Nag knew the business of mongooses, and was worried by Rikki-Tikki's appearance in the garden. It meant trouble for him and his family. "Let us talk about this," he said, hoping to distract Rikki-Tikki from his purpose. But Nag did not really want to discuss baby birds.

13 "Look out, Rikki-Tikki!" sang Darzee. Nagaina, Nag's wife, was trying to sneak up on the mongoose while her husband distracted him. Rikki-Tikki jumped as high as he could. When

he came down, he landed on Nagaina's back and bit her. But because he was still a young mongoose, he did not know how to kill her right away. Instead, he jumped back, and Nagaina escaped with her husband, hurt and angry but alive.

14   Rikki-Tikki was returning to the house when he saw Teddy playing outside. In the dirt nearby was a small brown snake. Because the snake was so much smaller than a cobra, no one was paying any attention to it. But this snake was just as dangerous as Nag, and Rikki-Tikki knew what he had to do. His eyes flamed red and he stood up on his back legs. The snake struck out at him, and soon they were fighting.

15   "Look! Our mongoose is killing a snake!" shouted Teddy. His parents came running from the house and arrived just as Rikki-Tikki gave the snake a final bite and won the battle. Teddy's father was very grateful, and his mother was so happy her boy was safe that she picked up Rikki-Tikki and hugged him! But Rikki-Tikki didn't understand what all the fuss was, because he was just having fun and doing his job. Besides, he knew that Nag and Nagaina were still alive.

16   That night, Nag and Nagaina were trying to decide what to do about Rikki-Tikki-Tavi.

17   "We must kill the people," Nagaina said. "They are the ones keeping the mongoose here. If they are gone, he will go, and we will have our garden back. We must make it safe for when our babies are born, and soon, because the eggs are about to hatch."

18   Nag agreed. "I will kill the big man, his wife, and the child," he said. He curled up around the bottom of a water jar to wait for the perfect chance, while Nagaina went to take care of her eggs. The two cobras did not know that Rikki-Tikki had found them while making his rounds through the garden. He had listened as they made their plan, getting angrier and angrier when he realized they were plotting to kill Teddy and his parents.

19   Rikki-Tikki waited, silently, until he was sure that Nagaina was gone and that Nag had fallen asleep by the water jar. As quietly as he could, he snuck over to where the big snake was sleeping and grabbed him behind his head. Nag woke up immediately and started shaking his head back and forth wildly, trying to throw Rikki-Tikki off. The mongoose was being beaten all over as the snake swung him around and around, but he refused to let go and sunk his teeth even further into Nag.

20   Suddenly, there was the sound of a gunshot, and Nag collapsed to the ground, as limp and lifeless as a piece of rope. Teddy's father had heard the noise of the fight and come out with his

gun. The man picked up Rikki-Tikki and turned to his frightened wife. "This mongoose has saved our lives!" he said.

21   Rikki-Tikki-Tavi rested that night, proud of himself for helping to defeat Nag. But he knew that his work was not finished, and that when the morning came, he would have to go searching for Nagaina and her eggs.

Digging Deeper

Rikki-Tikki-Tavi is the exciting story of a young and inexperienced mongoose who manages to defeat venomous snakes in battle. As we have discussed in this lesson, it is fiction, or a story that came from the imagination of the author. Sometimes, though, fiction is based on fact. What do you think? Could an animal like a mongoose *really* defeat one of the most dangerous snakes in the world in a fight?

FINDING MAIN IDEAS AND DETAILS

After reading "Rikki-Tikki-Tavi," answer the following questions.

1. Which sentence gives the **best summary** of the short story?

    A. A little boy and his parents find a sick young mongoose and nurse him back to health.

    B. A mongoose named Rikki-Tikki-Tavi partners with a bird named Darzee to kill an evil cobra named Nag.

    C. A family of humans is in danger from two cobras, Nag and Nagaina, who live in their garden.

    D. A mongoose named Rikki-Tikki-Tavi fights and kills snakes that threaten his human and animal friends.

2. In what **setting**, or time and place, does the story take place?

    _____

    _____

    _____

3. Which character(s) has/have eyes that "flamed red"?

    A. Darzee

    B. Rikki-Tikki-Tavi

    C. Nag and Nagaina

    D. Teddy's Father

4. Which quote from the story **best** explains why Teddy is allowed to keep Rikki-Tikki-Tavi?

    A. "But because mongooses are very curious, and the family had saved him and given him food, he was not scared of them."

    B. "But Rikki-Tikki didn't understand what all the fuss was, because he was just having fun and doing his job."

    C. 'Nonsense,' said the father. 'Our boy has never been safer. Mongooses can kill snakes, you know.'

    D. "Nag knew the business of mongooses, and was worried by Rikki-Tikki's appearance in the garden."

5. Place the following events in the correct order by giving each sentence a number from 1 to 5 so that 1 is the first event that happens and 5 is the last event.

   • Nag talks to Rikki-Tikki to distract him _____

   • Rikki-Tikki finds out who Nag is _____

   • Rikki-Tikki bites Nagaina _____

   • Nag and Nagaina eat one of Darzee's babies _____

   • Darzee warns Rikki-Tikki he is in danger _____

6. Using details from the story, describe Rikki-Tikki-Tavi the mongoose in complete sentences. Use your own words instead of copying the lines straight from the story! [*Hint:* Make sure you are using the details from the story, not the picture, to write your description!]

   _____

   _____

   _____

   _____

   _____

   _____

   _____

   _____

   _____

   _____

   _____

   _____

   _____

   _____

UNDERSTANDING TEXT STRUCTURE

After reading "Rikki-Tikki-Tavi," answer the following questions.

1. Look at the way "Rikki-Tikki-Tavi" is structured. Place a check mark next to each writing feature that you see.

_____ Sentences   _____ Stanzas   _____ Paragraphs

_____ Rhyming words   _____ Meter   _____ Dialogue
            (Conversations)

2. Now look at where you put your check marks and think about what you know about different kinds of writing, such as poetry. Is the story "Rikki-Tikki-Tavi" written in poetry?

A. Circle your response.

   Yes, the story is a poem.   No, the story is not a poem.

B. Why did you choose your response? Write your answer in complete sentences on the lines below.

_____

_____

_____

_____

_____

_____

_____

_____

_____

PROSE OR POETRY

In question 1, you probably placed a check mark by the words *sentences, paragraphs,* and *dialogue.* You probably left *verses, stanzas, rhyming words,* and *meter* blank.

Verses, stanzas, rhyming words, and meter are some of the elements that make poetry different from other types of writing. Poetry also has lines, and sometimes dialogue or even complete sentences, but it does not always include these things. Therefore, because "Rikki-Tikki-Tavi" does not have the special writing features that make poetry unique, we can conclude that it is not a poem that tells a short story. Instead, it is **prose**.

Prose is writing that reflects the way we usually talk and write. It uses sentences and paragraphs, instead of independent lines and stanzas. While dialogue, or conversation between two characters, can be included in both poetry and prose, it is often easier to find in prose.

Look back at the story and find some dialogue. How can you tell that the characters are talking?

UNDERSTANDING POINT OF VIEW

Another important part of reading a story is figuring out whose point of view it is written from. There are two main types that you will find in stories: **first person** and **third person**.

> In **first-person point of view**, the person telling the story, or narrator, is *inside* the story. The narrator is usually one of the main characters, or knows the main characters very well, and writes as if they personally are telling the reader what happened, using words like **"I"** and **"we."**
>
> In **third-person point of view**, the narrator is *outside* the story. The narrator is not one of the characters but describes what the characters are doing and saying, using words like **"he," "she," "it,"** and **"they."**

Now that you know a little more about point of view, let's apply it to "Rikki-Tikki-Tavi".

1. Who is the narrator of "Rikki-Tikki-Tavi"?

   A. Rikki-Tikki-Tavi

   B. Teddy's father

   C. Teddy

   D. None of the above

2. What point of view is "Rikki-Tikki-Tavi" written from?

   _____

   How do you know? Use an example from the text to support your answer.

   _____

   _____

   _____

   _____

   _____

Reading and Writing: Literature

CONNECTING LITERATURE AND ART

When "Rikki-Tikki-Tavi" was published as part of *The Jungle Book* in 1895, the book included illustrations. Use two of the illustrations, reproduced here, to answer the following questions.

1. Which sentence from the story is best illustrated by the picture?

   A. "When he came down, he landed on Nagaina's back and bit her."

   B. "It lifted the front part of its body completely off the ground and swayed back and forth like a dandelion tuft in the wind, ready to strike at any moment."

   C. "The mongoose was being beaten all over as the snake swung him around and around...."

   D. "His eyes flamed red and he stood up on his back legs. The snake struck out at him, and soon they were fighting."

2. Imagine that you have been asked to illustrate the next event in the story. In a complete sentence, describe what you would draw.

   _____

   _____

   _____

3. The story "Rikki-Tikki-Tavi" includes several snakes. Based on what you read, which snake do you think is pictured in the illustration on the right?

   A. Nag

   B. Nagaina

   C. The brown snake

   D. None of the above

The story you read is actually only the first *half* of the full story of "Rikki-Tikki-Tavi," and the illustration (right) is from the second half of the story, which you have not read.

4. Now that you have this new information, is your answer to question 3 different?

Yes _____   No _____

If you have a new answer, what is it? _____

Explain how you arrived at your answer (even if you did not need to change it):

_____

_____

_____

_____

_____

_____

UNDERSTANDING SIMILES

A simile uses the words *like* and *as* to compare two objects that are similar in some way. The comparison usually helps the reader "see" what is being described better than if the writer simply wrote the description without using a simile.

1. Which quote from the story is an example of a **simile**?

    A. "Rikki-Tikki jumped as high as he could."
    B. " ... and Nag collapsed to the ground, as limp and lifeless as a piece of rope."
    C. "His eyes flamed red and he stood up on his back legs."
    D. " ... and suddenly the head of a large cobra appeared, its wide hood spread threateningly."

2. Find another simile that is used in the story and write it in the space below. [*Hint:* There is one that describes Rikki-Tikki-Tavi and one that describes Nag.]

    _____

    _____

3. Consider the following short description from the story:

    "In the dirt nearby was a small brown snake."

    The sentence tells you that the snake is small and brown, but it does not add any detail. Use your imagination and your knowledge of similes to make the sentence more interesting and give a better description of the small brown snake in the space below.

    _____

    _____

4. Think about what you know about the character Nagaina. Practice writing similes of your own about her by filling in the blanks in the sentences below.

    A. Nagaina was as _____ as a/an _____

    _____

    B. Nagaina was _____ like _____

    _____

The Lady, or the Tiger?

1   A long time ago, there lived a powerful king. The king thought himself very smart, and wanted to show his people what a fair ruler he was. So, he built a large arena. Whenever a man broke the law, all of the king's subjects were gathered to the arena to see what would happen. The man who broke the law was then put in the center of the arena to wait for his sentence. But there were never any trials for these men. At least, not the normal sort of trials.

2   "Let there be two doors which open onto the arena floor," said the king, "and behind each door, a room, so well-built and protected that no sound can escape its walls. Before a judgment occurs, you must place a tiger in one of the rooms. In the other room, you must place a beautiful lady. Instead of judging the man, we will let fate decide. He must open the door of his choosing, never knowing which door **conceals** his life, and which his tomb. If the tiger comes out and **devours** him, we will know for certain that he was guilty of the crime. If, though, the lady comes out, he is innocent, and they should be married immediately."

3   The king thought that his idea was a very good one, because he could never be accused of judging someone wrongly. (He did not think about what should happen if the man was already married, or if the lawbreaker was a woman.) Besides, the people of the kingdom always thought it was exciting to come see a trial. Would it result in a death, or a wedding? No one ever knew how the play would end.

4   Now, the king had a beautiful daughter, the princess, who was the most prized jewel in the entire kingdom. The princess was in love with one of her father's noble and handsome subjects, and he loved her in return. But in those days, it was against the law for any man to fall in love with the princess, and when the king found out he was very angry at the young man who had been so bold as to love his daughter. Still, because he wanted to be a fair king, he could not simply feed the young man to the tiger. And so a day was set for his judgment. Like anyone else who broke the law, the young man would choose whether he lived to marry a beautiful lady or be eaten by a tiger.

5   Meanwhile, the princess was in **agony**. She had to find out which room would hold the tiger and which would hold the beautiful lady! No one had ever been able to find out the secret before. But the princess had enough money, and knew which people to ask. When the day of the trial came, she knew which room contained the tiger, and which held the beautiful lady. She even knew which lady it was—and she hated her, because if the young man chose her door, he would be forced to marry her instead of the princess.

6   In the arena, the princess sat beside her father, the king, watching the young man. The king's subjects also sat, all their eyes fixed on the young man. The lady and the tiger waited behind their doors. And the young man stood, a marble statue in the center of the arena. He stared at his princess, waiting for her to give him a sign. The princess slightly raised her right hand, but nobody except the young man noticed because they were all watching him, not the princess. As if released from a spell, the young man suddenly walked straight to the door on

the right, and opened it. And here is the point of our tale: Did the tiger come out of that door, or did the lady?

7   The princess knew that if she spared the young man's life by signaling the lady's door, she would have to watch him marry the lady she hated. They would never be together, and both of their hearts would be broken. But if she signaled for him to open the tiger's door, she would have to watch him be torn to death and eaten by the tiger. Which was the better fate—a death by marriage, or a death by tiger?

8   She had thought about what her decision must be for weeks, knowing that her beloved would expect her to have a sign for him. She had argued with herself back and forth, day and night, and when the day finally came she raised her hand on the right. But what was her final decision?

9   It is a difficult question, and I am certainly not the one person who can answer it. And so I leave it with all of you: Which came out of the opened door—the lady or the tiger?

glossary

agony: A very strong feeling of pain.

conceal: To keep something secret.

devour: To eat up greedily.

DETERMINING THEMES, CHARACTERS, AND CONCLUSIONS

Use "The Lady, or the Tiger?" to answer the following questions.

The theme of a piece of fiction is its view about life and how people behave. It is not directly presented in the text. You figure it out from the characters, action, and/or setting of the story. The theme is not intended to teach a lesson.

1. Based on what you read, which of the following sentences about the king is the **most** accurate?

   A. The king always did what was fair because he wanted the best for his subjects.

   B. Many of the things the king did were designed to make him look good to others.

   C. The king refused to judge his subjects because he was so smart that it would not have been fair to them.

   D. The main concern of the king was how to keep the princess safe from young men who broke the law.

2. In the last paragraph of the story, the narrator tells the reader that he is "not the one person who can answer" the question of the lady or the tiger. Who is the one person that can answer it?

   _____

   _____

3. What is the **theme**, or main idea, of the story?

   A. When humans let fate decide, the result is never really fair.

   B. People are usually not as smart as they think they are.

   C. Fear of the unknown can lead people to make poor decisions.

   D. In an impossible situation, there is no right answer.

4. Which character does the princess become **most** upset with?

   A. Her father, the king

   B. The tiger

   C. The lady

   D. The young man

5. Which of the following sentences **best** summarizes how the king's subjects feel about the trial system?

   A. The subjects find the trials interesting no matter if the person on trial lives or dies.

   B. The subjects know that the king is just trying to make himself look good, but they go along with it anyway.

   C. The subjects think that the trials are pointless because there is no real judgment happening, just chance.

   D. The subjects enjoy the trials but worry what will happen if a person who is already married ends up choosing the lady.

6. What information does the princess go looking for in the story?

   _____

   _____

   _____

   _____

   How does she find it?

   _____

   _____

   _____

   _____

7. What do your answers from question 6 tell you about the character of the princess? Be sure to use your own words, and write your answer in complete sentences.

   _____

   _____

   _____

   _____

   _____

   _____

UNDERSTANDING METAPHORS

A **metaphor** is a type of figurative language, similar to a simile. Like a simile, it makes a comparison that draws a word picture for the reader. However, although a simile uses the words "like" and "as," a metaphor does not.

Use "The Lady, or the Tiger?" to answer the following questions.

1. Which of the following sentences from the story contains a metaphor?

    A. "Like anyone else who broke the law, the young man would choose whether he lived to marry a beautiful lady or be eaten by a tiger."

    B. "Now, the king had a beautiful daughter, the princess, who was the most prized jewel in the entire kingdom."

    C. "When the day of the trial came, she knew which room contained the tiger, and which held the beautiful lady."

    D. "If the tiger comes out and devours him, we will know for certain that he was guilty of the crime."

2. What **metaphor** is used in paragraph 6? Fill in the blanks provided with your answer. Be careful! There is also a simile in the paragraph.

    In paragraph 6, a/the _____ is compared to a/the

    _____.

    What does the metaphor let you, the reader, know about the subject of the comparison? [*Hint:* The subject of the metaphor is probably what you wrote in the first space. It is the person or object that is being described by the metaphor.]

    _____

    _____

    _____

    _____

3. Consider this sentence from paragraph 2:

   "*He must open the door of his choosing, never knowing which door conceals his life, and which his tomb.*"

   Based on your knowledge of the story, fill in the blanks in the following sentence:

   The doors that the young man must choose from do not actually conceal "his life" and "his

   tomb." Instead, "his tomb" is a metaphor for the _____ ,

   whereas "his life" is a metaphor that replaces the _____ .

4. Which of the following sentences best explains this metaphor of **a play** that is found in the story?

   "*Besides, the people of the kingdom always thought it was exciting to come see a trial. Would it result in a death, or a wedding? No one ever knew how **the play** would end.*"

   A. The comparison of the trial to a play tells the reader that the people in the kingdom thought that it was all a big show and that no one was actually getting killed or married.

   B. The comparison of the trial to a play tells the reader that the king thought of the trials as a game and has been using his subjects as his toys all along.

   C. The comparison of the trial to a play tells the reader that the narrator of the story is not taking it seriously and is just asking the question to play with the minds of his readers.

   D. The comparison of the trial to a play tells the reader that the subjects of the kingdom saw the trials as a kind of entertainment to enjoy, instead of a matter of life and death.

WRITE YOUR OPINION

The narrator of "The Lady, or the Tiger?" claimed that he could not answer the question at the end of the story. Can you?

Imagine that you are a detective. You have been asked to solve the mystery of "The Lady, or the Tiger?" and determine which one came through the door—or, to put it another way, which ending the princess chose for the young man. Which one did she pick, and why did she decide that way?

As a detective, you know there are several steps you need to follow in your investigation.

1. First, you will have to gather your "clues" and "evidence" from the short story. Sometimes, there are clues that seem to point to opposite answers. Still, it can be helpful to find both. Use the chart provided to organize the evidence you find in the story. Think about what you know about the princess's personality, thoughts, and actions. Write down as much as you can in each column!

The princess might have chosen the tiger because . . .	The princess might have chosen the lady because . . .

2. Now that you have gathered your evidence for both options, look over your "clues" carefully and make your decision.

Things you may want to consider:

- Does one column have more evidence in it than the other?
- Do the clues on one side seem more significant?
- Can you explain one choice better than the other?

Once you have made your decision, write it in the space provided.

3. You have been informed that, as the lead detective on the case, it will be your responsibility to write an official report stating your opinion of the case. In order for the report to be complete, you must have at least three reasons or pieces of evidence for your decision. Write your three reasons on the lines provided.

Reason 1: _____

_____

_____

_____

_____

Reason 2: _____

_____

_____

_____

_____

Reason 3: _____

_____

_____

_____

_____

Now you are ready to write your report!

- First, you will need a topic sentence where you state your opinion.

- Next, include the three (or more) reasons for your opinion. Remember to link your reasons together with phrases like "in addition" or "for instance."

- The last part of your report should be a conclusion that brings the whole report together and restates your opinion.

You can use the provided template to get started!

Case No. 1882	"The Lady, or the Tiger?" as reported by Mr. Frank Stockton
Date:	Filing Detective:

Having completed a thorough investigation of the facts in the case, "The Lady, or the Tiger?" it is my professional opinion that the door chosen by the princess …

_____

_____

_____

_____

_____

_____

_____

_____

_____

_____

_____

_____

UNIT 8

Poetry

A poem is a piece of writing that can express an idea or an emotion, describe an object, or even tell a story. A poem can be about almost anything, and there are many different kinds of poetry. Some poems have rhyme and rhythm, and others do not. Poems can be as short as a few words or as long as an entire book. But since poems can be so different from each other, how can you tell if you are reading a poem and not prose, or writing that is not poetry? In this unit, you will practice reading poetry and identifying some of the things that make poetry special.

An Emerald is as Green as Grass

By Christina Rossetti (1872)

An emerald is as green as grass;
A ruby red as blood;
A sapphire shines as blue as heaven;
A flint lies in the mud.
A diamond is a brilliant stone,
To catch the world's desire;
An opal holds a fiery spark;
But a flint holds fire.

EXPAND YOUR KNOWLEDGE:

Emeralds, rubies, sapphires, diamonds, and opals are known as gems, or precious stones, because they are beautiful, hard to find, and worth a lot of money. They are often used to make beautiful jewelry. Flint is a kind of stone that is not as pretty as a gemstone. However, when flint is struck against steel, a spark of fire is made. Long before people had matches, lighters, or electricity, they could use a flint and steel to start fires for cooking or keeping warm.

DRAWING CONCLUSIONS AND UNDERSTANDING DETAILS

Use "An Emerald is as Green as Grass" to answer the following questions.

1. Which sentence would be an example of a **detail** from the poem?

   A. Flints are the same color as mud.

   B. Sapphires are blue and shiny.

   C. Opals and flints are both fiery stones.

   D. Flints are more important than diamonds.

2. Which stone is the same color as the sky?

   A. ruby

   B. emerald

   C. diamond

   D. sapphire

Sometimes, the key idea is stated directly in the writing. Other times, the reader must make an inference, or use the details to figure out what the writer is saying.

3. Which sentence would be an example of an **inference** that a reader could make about flint?

   A. Flints are often found in the mud.

   B. Flints are more like opals than any other stone.

   C. Flints should not be compared to more colorful stones.

   D. Flints are not beautiful, but they are still important.

4. Consider one inference that can be made from the poem: "People usually think diamonds are worth more than flints." What details from the poem would you use to support this inference? List at least two.

   A. _____

   B. _____

Now that you have identified some details from the text and made an inference, let's put it all together! As you learned earlier, the main idea, or theme, is what the entire piece of writing is about. Sometimes, it is a message that the writer is trying to tell to the reader.

5. What is the **theme**, or message of the poem, "An Emerald is as Green as Grass?"

   A. Things that are pretty are almost always useless.

   B. Beauty is not the only thing that gives an object value.

   C. The value of a stone cannot be determined from its color.

   D. If a stone can be used to create fire, it is worth more than gems.

FINDING CONTEXT CLUES AND CONSULTING REFERENCE MATERIALS

Reread the poem, "An Emerald is as Green as Grass," and answer this next set of questions. Read these sentences from the poem:

*A diamond is a **brilliant** stone,*
*To catch the world's **desire**;*

Now look at these dictionary entries for the word *brilliant*:

1: very bright

2: very impressive or successful

3: much more intelligent than most people

1. Which sentences use the word **brilliant** as the first line shown above? Circle <u>all</u> that apply.

   A. Troy is a brilliant student in literature.

   B. Emmanuel gave a brilliant performance at his music concert.

   C. The sun was so brilliant that not even sunglasses could protect my eyes.

   D. Tatianna wrote a brilliant poem that won first place in the state poetry contest.

Next, look at this dictionary entry for the word *desire*:

1. : to long or hope for

2. : to express a wish for

2. Which sentence uses the word **desire** as the second line shown on the previous page? Circle <u>all</u> that apply.

   A. Athena's desire is to graduate college with a degree in medicine.

   B. Mr. Yanni desires all of his students to receive the best education possible.

   C. Hayden's desire is for his family to help with his school's fundraising efforts.

   D. Eli desires a quick answer from his teacher to know if he passed his literature test.

LEARNING THE STRUCTURE OF POEMS AND PROSE

What makes a poem—a poem?

As you learned at the beginning of the unit, there are different ways to tell whether a piece of writing is a poem or not. Poems come in all shapes and sizes. Look at the structure of the writing. This refers to how the writing is put together. Many poems have a structure that is different from prose.

Stanzas

For example, poems often have sections. Each section is called a **stanza**, or verse. In each verse, there are lines. Sometimes the lines in a verse *rhyme*, or use words that have similar sounds at the end of the line.

Meter (rhythm)

Lines and verses can also have a **meter**, or **rhythm**, so that reading them is almost like singing a song. Meter is all about the rhythm that the entire line makes. Poets create this type of rhythm by paying attention to how many *syllables* each line of poetry has and how the syllables are read. Often, a poem will have both rhyme and rhythm!

> "Mrs. Spot likes to *cook*, my friends and I want to *look*
> What is in your big tan *pot*? May we have some Mrs. *Spot*?"

Alliteration

Now take a look at this sentence:

> "The **b**ig **b**lue **b**all **b**ounced over the **b**abbling **b**rook."

Did you see anything unique about it? As you probably noticed, the "b" sound is repeated so that when the sentence is read out loud, the words seem to bounce just like the ball: "The **b**ig **b**lue **b**all **b**ounced over the **b**abbling **b**rook."

This repetition of sounds is called **alliteration** and is often used in poetry along with rhyme and rhythm to create a word picture for the reader.

Use "An Emerald is as Green as Grass" to answer the following questions.

1. What two words does the poet rhyme in the second verse?

    _____ and _____

2. List two examples of **alliteration** from the poem.

    A. _____

    B. _____

3. Read the following line from the poem:

    "An opal holds a fiery spark."

    Which part of a poem's structure does the line show when it is written this way?

    A. A stanza

    B. Alliteration

    C. Meter

    D. A syllable

4. Did the writer of this poem use syllables to create **meter**? Explain.

    _____

    _____

UNDERSTANDING SIMILES

Imagine you have just come home from a trip to a faraway place. Your friends ask you what it was like, but you don't have any pictures to show them. What could you do? Make a word picture, of course! You would have to describe the things that you saw, heard, touched, smelled, tasted, and felt.

Writers do the same thing for their readers. One way that many writers make a word picture is by using figurative language. Figurative language is language that helps the reader "see" what the writer "sees" or feel what the writer feels by comparing it to something that the reader already understands. As you learned in a previous lesson, one type of figurative language that many writers and poets use is a **simile**. A simile is a comparison that uses the words *like* or *as* to make a word picture more powerful.

> **Read these sentences:**
>
> "The girl's hair was brown and gold."
>
> "The girl's hair was brown and gold like autumn leaves."
>
> "The boy's face was pale."
>
> "The boy's face was as pale as a piece of paper."

Which sentences help you make a better picture in your mind? Most likely, it was the second ones...the similes!

Use the poem from the beginning of the lesson to answer these questions:

1. Which line from the poem is an example of a **simile**?

   A. "A flint lies in the mud"

   B. "An opal holds a fiery spark"

   C. "A diamond is a brilliant stone"

   D. "An emerald is as green as grass"

2. What other examples of similes can you find in the poem?

   A. _____

   B. _____

3. Rewrite one of the similes from the poem so that it is just a regular describing sentence, not a simile. *(Hint:* It will probably be much shorter!)

_____

_____

_____

4. Look at the regular sentence you just wrote and the simile that it came from. How are they the same?

_____

_____

_____

How are they different?

_____

_____

_____

Which one gives a better description?

_____

_____

_____

Why?

_____

_____

Digging Deeper

Is an emerald really as green as grass? Find out! With the help of an adult, search the Internet. Try to find each of the stones mentioned in the poem. Which one is your favorite? Can you create some similes of your own to describe the other stones?

Fog
By Carl Sandburg (1916)

The fog comes on
little cat feet.

It sits looking
over harbor and city
on silent haunches and
then moves on.

DRAWING CONCLUSIONS AND UNDERSTANDING DETAILS

"Fog" is an example of a *free-verse* poem, meaning it does not rhyme or have a rhythm like many poems do. However, it does have lines and stanzas, and paints a word picture for the reader, just like "An Emerald is as Green as Grass."

Use "Fog" to answer the following questions.

1. Which statement **best summarizes** the second stanza of the poem?

    A. A cat that is looking at a foggy city and harbor gets up and walks away.
    B. The city and harbor are covered in fog, and then the fog goes away.
    C. Fog comes into a city like a cat, covers the city and the harbor, and then disappears.
    D. Cats move quietly, just like the fog that comes into a city and quietly disappears.

2. Based on the details in the poem, what two things are being compared?

    A. Fog and quiet cities
    B. Fog and cat feet
    C. Cats and foggy cities
    D. Cats and fog

3. Which sentence states the **main idea**, or **theme**, of the poem?

    A. Cats can be compared to fog moving quietly through a city.
    B. City life is similar to a cat moving through the fog.
    C. The way fog moves through a city is similar to the way a cat moves.
    D. Cats and fog both move through cities and harbors quietly.

4. One way that a writer can add detail to a poem is by using adjectives, or describing words. Find two adjectives in "Fog" and use them to complete the provided chart.

Adjective (Describing Word)	What Word Is It Describing?

Challenge: How does the detail given by the adjectives you found affect the poem?
(*Hint:* **Think about how the poem would be different if the describing words were not there or even if the opposite describing word was used!**)

_____

_____

UNDERSTANDING METAPHORS

Metaphors paint powerful word pictures, but they can be harder to find, because they do not use certain words such as *like* and *as* to make comparisons. Instead, a metaphor compares two things by saying that one thing **is** the other. The two things being compared are not exactly the same, but making it sound like they are creates a stronger word picture for the reader.

> **Read these sentences:**
>
> "The red ruby was sitting on the white cloth."
>
> "The ruby was as red as blood sitting on the white cloth."
>
> "The ruby was a drop of blood sitting on the white cloth."
>
> "The woman's hair was shoulder-length and white."
>
> "The woman's hair was shoulder-length and white like a cloud."
>
> "The woman's hair was a shoulder-length white cloud."

As you probably noticed, the first sentence in each group did not use any figurative language. The second sentence in each group was a simile and made a comparison using *like* or *as*. The third sentence made the same comparison as the second sentence but did not use the words *like* or *as*. Those are the metaphors!

Now that you understand what a metaphor is, reread "Fog" for a second time and answer the following questions:

1. Which sentence correctly states the metaphor that is used in "Fog"? (*Hint:* It may be helpful to look back at your answers from the last section of this lesson!)

    A. The movement of fog is being used as a metaphor for the movement of a cat.

    B. The movement of a cat is being used as a metaphor for the movement of fog.

    C. The movement of a cat in the fog is being used as a metaphor for a quiet city.

    D. The movement of fog in a city is being used as a metaphor for quiet cat feet.

2. If you were asked to rewrite the poem as a single sentence but still keep the metaphor, which sentence would be correct?

    A. The fog is a cat that quietly comes into a city, stays for a little while, and then leaves.

    B. The fog comes into the city as quietly as a cat, stays for a little while, and then leaves.

    C. The fog is moving through the city the same way a cat moves, quietly.

    D. The fog moves into a city the same way it leaves, quietly and like a cat.

3. Rewrite the metaphor from "Fog" as a simile in the space below. (*Hint:* There is more than one way you can do this!)

    _____

    _____

    _____

4. Now, take the simile and rewrite it as a regular sentence, without figurative language.

    _____

    _____

    _____

5. Look at the two sentences you just wrote plus the original poem, "Fog." Do all of the sentences give you the same basic information about fog? Why or why not?

    _____

    _____

    _____

6. Which one has the most detail: the metaphor poem, the simile sentence, or the regular sentence?

_____

_____

7. Which one would be the easiest to draw or describe to someone?

_____

_____

Why?

_____

_____

WRITE YOUR OPINION

When Carl Sandburg saw fog move into his city and then go away, he was apparently reminded of a cat. How about you? Does the weather ever remind you of an animal? Consider some types of weather.

Sunshine

Thunderstorm

Rain shower

Hail

Wind

Heat wave

Hurricane

Tornado

Snow

Other

Circle the type of weather that reminds you of an animal. Be creative! It can be any animal that you can think of. However, you need to be able to explain why that type of weather and animal are similar. Think about how they act, how they make you feel, and what they look, smell, and sound like. Remember, this is your opinion, and other people do not have to agree with it, but you do have to be able to support it!

Have you thought of anything yet? Write it in the space provided.

A/The _____ (weather) reminds me of a/an _____ (animal) because...

Reason 1: _____

_____

_____

_____

Reason 2: _____

_____

_____

_____

Reason 3: _____

_____

_____

_____

Now you are ready! Imagine that you can send a letter back in time to Carl Sandburg. You want to tell him what kind of animal the weather reminds you of. You will want to make sure that your letter includes a greeting and lets Mr. Sandburg know who you are and why you are writing to him.

Then, write your opinion paragraph. You will need a topic sentence where you state your opinion. Next, include the three or more reasons for your opinion. Remember to link your reasons together with phrases like "because," "in addition," or "for instance." The last part of your opinion paragraph should be a conclusion that brings the whole paragraph together and restates your opinion.

Finally, end your letter with a phrase such as "Sincerely," or "Your Friend," and add your signature. Your opinion letter is complete!

REVIEW

Reading Poetry

In Unit 8, you learned about some of the special features of poetry that make it different from other types of writing. Practice reading the following poem out loud with an adult. As you read, pay attention to the syllables and how the words are arranged. This will help you find the meter, or rhythm, of the poem. Also, pay attention to how the words are used in the poem. Are there any words that you do not recognize or that are being used in an unfamiliar way? Write them down in the space provided!

Blowing Bubbles

By William Allingham (1909)

See, the pretty Planet!
    Floating sphere!
Faintest breeze will fan it,
    Far or near;
World as light as feather;
    Moonshine rays,
Rainbow tints together,
    As it plays;
Drooping, sinking, failing,
    Nigh to earth,
Mounting, whirling, sailing,
    Full of mirth;
Life there, welling, flowing,
    Waving round;
Pictures coming, going,
    Without sound.
Quick now, be this airy
    Globe repell'd!
Never can the fairy
    Star be held.
Touch'd—it in a twinkle
    Disappears!
Leaving but a sprinkle,
    As of tears.

Write the unfamilar words here.

_____
_____
_____
_____
_____
_____
_____
_____
_____
_____

Activity 1

Use "Blowing Bubbles" to answer the next set of questions. How did you do? Were there any words you did not know? How about these words:

Nigh   Mirth   Welling   Airy

1. Figure out what these words mean using **context clues**, or looking at the surrounding words that you do know. Your definition should fit with the rest of the verse. Use the lines provided for your definitions:

   A. Nigh _____

   B. Mirth _____

   C. Welling _____

   D. Airy _____

2. Now, use a dictionary to look up each word. You may need to ask an adult for help, especially if you are using an online dictionary. Some of the words may have multiple definitions listed, so make sure you find the one that makes the most sense with the rest of the verse. Write what you find in the space below. (*Hint:* "Welling" will be listed under the verb entry for the word "well." Remember, a verb is an action word.)

   A. Nigh _____

   B. Mirth _____

   C. Welling _____

   D. Airy _____

You can use this same process with any other unfamiliar words in the poem or with unfamiliar words in anything you read.

Now that you have a better understanding of the words, read the poem again. This time, see if you can find the meter of the words. Since this is the second time you are reading the poem, it will probably be a lot easier!

Activity 2

Use "Blowing Bubbles" to answer the questions below.

1. Which phrase from the poem is a metaphor for the bubble?
   A. "airy globe"
   B. "rainbow tints"
   C. "pretty Planet"
   D. "floating sphere"

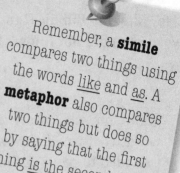

Remember, a **simile** compares two things using the words <u>like</u> and <u>as</u>. A **metaphor** also compares two things but does so by saying that the first thing <u>is</u> the second thing.

2. Can you find any other metaphors for the bubble? Write at least one on the lines below.

   _____

   _____

3. Which lines from the poem contain a simile?
   A. "Rainbow tints together / As it plays"
   B. "Never can the fairy / Star be held"
   C. "Mounting, whirling, sailing / Full of mirth"
   D. "Leaving but a sprinkle / As of tears"

Both similes and metaphors are types of figurative language, or language that helps the reader better see what the writer is describing

4. There is another simile in the poem that actually uses three objects! Can you find it? Fill in the blanks in the following sentence with your answers:

   The bubble is described as being as _____ as a/an _____

   or a/an _____ .

5. In question 4, the bubble is the subject of the simile, the object being described.

   Now, create a new simile that compares the two objects of the simile, or things the bubble was being compared to. [*Hint:* One of the objects from the first simile needs to become the subject for the new simile, and the bubble will not be mentioned at all! There are two possible ways for you to do this.]

   _____

   _____

   _____

UNDERSTAND

Let's apply the reading skills you covered in this section.

1. What event occurs in the last stanza of the poem?

   _____

2. Which statement **best** summarizes the poem?

   A. A child blowing bubbles touches one of them, and when the bubble pops, the child starts to cry.

   B. A bubble floats through the air, moving up and down and all around, until someone touches it and it pops.

   C. A bubble floating through the air is picked up by the wind, which eventually sends it down to the ground, where it pops.

   D. A child blowing bubbles imagines that they are little planets with tiny people and fairies living on them, until the bubble pops.

3. Place the actions of the bubble in the poem in the correct order by numbering the following statements from 1 to 4, where 1 is the first thing that happens and 4 is the last thing that happens.

   A. The bubble rises up in the sky _____

   B. The bubble pops _____

   C. The bubble moves away from the narrator _____

   D. The bubble comes closer to the ground _____

4. You can use the details in a poem to determine the mood, or "feel," of the piece. How would you describe the mood for most of this poem? Write your answer in complete sentences, and make sure you support your answer with details from the poem.

   _____

   _____

5. Does the mood change at all in the poem? Explain why or why not, using details from the poem.

   _____

DISCOVER

Write Your Opinion

You have practiced writing your opinion for two imaginary situations. Now, let's review the steps and practice writing an opinion piece for a real-world audience.

The Great Bubble Debate

Your school has the option of participating in a research project. Some scientists are trying to see whether blowing bubbles is really good for you, like experts say. They would like to provide all of the students and teachers with blowing bubbles and have two 5-minute bubble-blowing breaks every day for one month—one break in the morning and one in the afternoon.

The scientists want to see if the students feel more relaxed and are able to focus better if they take time to blow bubbles. They also want to see if teachers notice a difference in how their students behave or how much teaching they are able to do. Finally, they want to look at a month's worth of student grades before the bubble experiment and compare them to grades earned during the experiment to see if there might be academic benefit to taking bubble breaks.

Your principal would like the school to participate in the study but first must get approval by at least seventy-five percent, or three-fourths, of the students and their parents. She has asked each student to submit a letter stating his or her opinion and the reasons why they would, or would not, like to participate in the study.

From what you have learned about opinion writing, you know that you will need to:

• Research the topic
• Form your opinion, based on your prior knowledge and your research

You probably already know a little bit about bubble blowing and how it makes people feel from your personal experience. Opinions can be based completely on feelings, but it is usually good to include facts as well. With the help of an adult, do some research about bubble blowing.

Many resources are written for adult readers, so there will probably be words that you do not understand. However, by using context clues, looking up unfamiliar words, and asking for help when you need it, you will be able to find interesting facts to help you reach your opinion.

Remember, you can use any information you would like to make your opinion, in addition to the links provided. When you are writing an opinion piece, there is no right or wrong answer, as long as you can explain why you feel the way you do!

1. Sometimes when you are making a decision, it is helpful to make a list of pros and cons. Fill in the chart below with as many pros and cons as you can think of. Be creative! Although there are some pros and cons that may be obvious, there are probably some that only you can think of, too!

5-Minute Bubble Breaks at School	
Pros	**Cons**

Just as you did with "The Lady, or the Tiger?" evaluate your list of pros and cons and decide whether you are for or against the bubble-blowing program.

2. Now that you know what your opinion is, write down at least three reasons you can use to support it. If you are using a reason that is based on something you read in the poem or on a website, make sure you cite it, or give credit to where the information came from. However, make sure that you put your reasons in your own words instead of just copying them straight from the source!

Reason 1:

_____

_____

_____

Reason 2:

_____

_____

_____

Reason 3:

_____

_____

_____

Reason 4 (optional):

_____

_____

_____

Now you are ready to write your opinion letter! You will need to begin with a greeting, letting the principal know who you are and why you are writing (you will probably state your opinion here). Then, explain your opinion using the reasons you listed above. Conclude your opinion letter with a restatement of your opinion and a respectful closing salutation, such as "Sincerely," or "Regards." Finally, sign your name. Your letter is complete!

Mythology and Fables

A *myth* is a traditional story that teaches a lesson, tells why something happened, or explains the unexplainable in a way for people to understand. Myths use supernatural characters and events, like gods, goddesses, spirits, and curses.

Fables are short stories that teach a moral or a lesson. Many fables have been passed down over centuries of time through different generations of people. The characters in fables are usually animals that are given human qualities. Children of all ages enjoy fables. A very well-known fable storyteller is *Aesop*—the ancient Greek storyteller. Not much is known about him. Some sources say he was a slave who lived in 6 B.C. Others say he did not exist at all but that the name "Aesop" was given to a group of fables that used animals as characters. These fables all have a moral, or type of theme that teaches a lesson.

In this unit you will read some well-known myths and a fable to practice your reading, writing, and vocabulary skills.

Pandora's Box

1 I am Pandora, the first woman created by Zeus, king of the gods. The world I was brought into was perfect and knew no hardships. On my wedding day, Zeus presented me with a beautiful box made of dark wood with gold hinges. A gold key was inserted into its latch with a note tied on it that read, "Do not open."

2 The note made me want to open the box all the more. Every night, I lay awake and wondered about this mysterious box. My curiosity gnawed at me like a hungry creature. What could be in it? If I could only take one quick peep, I would be satisfied! How would Zeus even know if I opened its lid?

3 One night, I could not control my curiosity any longer. I crept downstairs and gazed at the beautiful box. The gold hinges glittered against the flame of my candle. My fingers trembled as I touched the key. What if Zeus was watching me? My hand whipped back as if a snake had bitten me. I looked behind me, but I was alone. I laughed at my foolishness and turned back to the box. I gripped the key more firmly and turned it slowly until I heard a loud click. The box was unlocked! I held my breath as my hands slowly lifted both sides of its lid.

4 Suddenly, a thousand hardships flew past me like an angry swarm of wasps. I slammed the lid tight to keep them from escaping, but it was too late. Everything bad—war, disease, hunger, pain, gossip, anger, envy, hate, illness, and so many others—had now escaped into the world, and it was my fault!

5 "Why did you not listen to me?" I heard the voice of Zeus say from behind.

6 "Oh, Zeus," I sobbed as I turned around and saw him standing before me. "Can I ever be forgiven?"

7 "I can forgive you, Pandora, but I cannot make these awful hardships return to the box. From now on, the world will suffer from your actions." He shook his head. "But do not cry so, for you were able to trap the most important thing."

8 "What is that?" I asked.

9 "Hope," he replied, smiling. "You still have hope. Just remember that no matter how terrible things may seem from now on, there will always be hope to hold onto."

Digging Deeper

Myths are stories with vivid visual details. Tell the Pandora story or another ancient myth through a series of pictures. You can draw pictures, download free art from the Internet (with an adult's supervision), or cut out images from old newspapers or magazines. See if others can tell what happens in the story without using any words in your picture book.

DETERMINING THEMES

Use "Pandora's Box" to answer the following questions.

1. What is the **central message** of the story?

   A. Open a mysterious box only if you know what is inside of it.

   B. Leave a mysterious box alone unless you are told to open it.

   C. Ignore a warning sign if you have a desire to know something.

   D. Follow a warning sign, or others may suffer from your actions.

> The theme or central message is the subject of a story. A good reader can give a short statement to tell what the story is about.

2. Which statement **best** tells what the story is about?

   A. Zeus gives Pandora a box as a gift, and hope remains inside it.

   B. Pandora releases all hardships into the world, but hope remains.

   C. Zeus gives Pandora a mysterious box and tells her never to open it.

   D. Pandora is forgiven for releasing all the hardships into the world.

DESCRIBING CHARACTERS, SETTINGS, AND EVENTS

1. Which detail from the story **best** describes Pandora's character?

   A. "My curiosity gnawed at me like a hungry creature."

   B. "I crept downstairs and gazed at the beautiful box."

   C. "My hand whipped back as if a snake had bitten me."

   D. "I held my breath as my hands slowly lifted both sides of its lid."

> How a character thinks, feels, or acts are the most important parts of a story. The setting helps the reader know where the story is taking place. Events are created by the action in the story.

2. Which of the following is the **most** important event of the story?

   A. Pandora's fingers shake as she touches the key to the box.

   B. Pandora stays awake every night and thinks about the box.

   C. The hardships fly out of the box before Pandora can stop them.

   D. The gold on the box glitters when Pandora holds up the candle.

DETERMINING THE MEANING OF PHRASES

Stories, particularly myths, often have words or phrases where you need to determine the meaning. Some phrases from myths carry a special meaning and are still used today.

Use "Pandora's Box" to answer the following questions.

1. The story of Pandora's box is very well known. Even today, people still use the phrase, "That person has opened a Pandora's box." What do you think this phrase means? Choose details from the story to support your answer.

_____

_____

_____

_____

_____

_____

_____

2. What does the sentence, "There will always be hope to hold onto," mean? Use details from the story to support your answer.

_____

_____

_____

_____

_____

_____

_____

USING COMMAS AND QUOTATION MARKS

Use quotation marks to set off a direct quotation of spoken language. A quotation is set off from the rest of the sentence by a comma. Periods and commas always go inside of the quotation marks.

> ### Examples:
>
> Miyang Ling said, "I like learning about mythology."
>
> "So do I," said Sandeep.
>
> "My favorite character is Atlas," Alana replied.

Insert commas and quotation marks into each of the following sentences.

1. Because my curiosity was so strong said Pandora I had to open the box.

2. If you had followed the note Zeus responded then the world would still be free of hardships.

3. I am very sorry Pandora cried.

4. You are forgiven Zeus smiled.

The Trojan Horse

The Trojan soldiers **peered** over the high wall they were guarding. They could not believe their eyes! A huge wooden horse with wheels for hooves was in front of the gates to the city of Troy. How did it get there? To whom did it belong?

A single Greek soldier stood next to the horse. The Trojan soldiers were very curious.

Who was this man? Why was he alone? Where did the rest of the Greek army go? For ten long years the Trojan people had defended their city against the Greeks. The war had started when the wife of the king of Sparta was taken from Greece to Troy. Some say she was kidnapped, and others say she went willingly. The Greeks wanted her back, but the Trojans wanted her to stay, so the war continued.

A small band of Trojan soldiers marched through the **sturdy** gates of Troy and approached the lone Greek. "Who are you?" they asked.

"My name is Sinon," the Greek solider replied. "The whole Greek army has sailed back to Greece. I was left here to offer this fine wooden horse to the goddess Athena, in return for their safe passage."

The Trojan soldiers looked at the horse and whispered among themselves. Why should the Greeks have this fine horse to offer to Athena? They could give this gift to her themselves! They wheeled it into the city of Troy, although it was almost too tall to pass through the gates. By the time they wheeled the horse in, it was nightfall. They decided to go to sleep and offer it to Athena the next day.

Once the whole city of Troy was asleep, a small door under the belly of the horse opened slowly. A long ladder of rope was swiftly lowered to the ground. Within minutes, thirty Greek soldiers scrambled down the ladder and were out of the horse. Their leader Odysseus, the quick-witted warrior who thought of this plan to fool the Trojans, motioned his men to the gates. They crept to the large doors and scaled up the side of the walls to unlock them. Then they quickly flung open the gates, allowing the whole Greek army, which had by that time assembled outside, to rush into the city of Troy. They attacked the Trojan soldiers in their sleep and captured Troy before sunrise.

By morning, the city of Troy had fallen to Greece, the war was over, and Helen was sailing back to her home in Sparta. Odysseus was hailed as a hero for thinking of the plan to use the wooden horse, and the Trojan army was very upset at being so easily fooled by the Greeks.

glossary

peered: Looked, stared.

sturdy: Strong, firm.

DETERMINING THEMES

Use "The Trojan Horse" to answer the following questions.

1. What is the "The Trojan Horse" **mainly** about?

    A. The Greek soldiers offered a wooden horse as a gift to Athena so that she would give them safe passage home.

    B. The Greek army won the war by tricking the Trojans into taking the wooden horse in the city.

    C. The Trojan soldiers took the wooden horse so that they could offer it as a gift to Athena.

    D. The Trojan army fought a war for several years until the Greeks built a wooden horse.

2. What is the **theme** of this story?

    A. Gifts do not always mean something.

    B. Always give your enemy a gift to win a fight.

    C. Be careful of gifts that come from your enemy.

    D. Always offer a gift to someone who will keep you safe.

USING DETAILS AND EXAMPLES

1. Why were the Greeks and Trojans at war?

    A. Helen had been taken to Troy, and the Greeks wanted her back.

    B. Odysseus wanted to show the Greek army how to fool its enemy.

    C. Sinon had fooled the Trojans into thinking the wooden horse was for them.

    D. Athena wanted the Greeks to get back the wooden horse from the Trojans.

2. Which sentence from the story supports the idea that tricking the Trojans was a good idea?

    A. "The Trojan soldiers peered over the high wall they were guarding."

    B. "Trojan soldiers looked at the horse and whispered among themselves."

    C. "A small band of Trojan soldiers marched through the sturdy gates of Troy and approached the lone Greek."

    D. "They attacked the Trojan soldiers in their sleep and captured Troy before sunrise."

COMPARING AND CONTRASTING POINTS OF VIEW

After you have read "Pandora's Box" and "The Trojan Horse," use details from each text to complete the following activity.

1. How are the points of view in the stories the same?

Pandora's Box	The Trojan Horse

2. How are the points of view in the story different?

Pandora's Box	The Trojan Horse

3. Which story uses **first person** in its narration? Which uses **third person**? Write a sentence from the story that uses an example of what point of view is being used for each story.

   A. First person

   Story title: _____

   Example from story: _____

   _____

   B. Third person

   Story title: _____

   Example from story: _____

   _____

First-person writing is from the point of view of the author. You will read pronouns such as **I**, **me**, **us**, and **we** in first person writing.

Third-person writing tells about someone or something else. Authors use names or pronouns such as **he**, **it**, or **they**.

COMPARING AND CONTRASTING THEMES

Read both "Pandora's Box" and "The Trojan Horse," and complete the following activity.

The events in a piece of writing will shape its theme. Compare and contrast the events in the stories. Write the events that are similar in the center of the Venn diagram. Write how they are different under each story title. Use details from the text to support your answers.

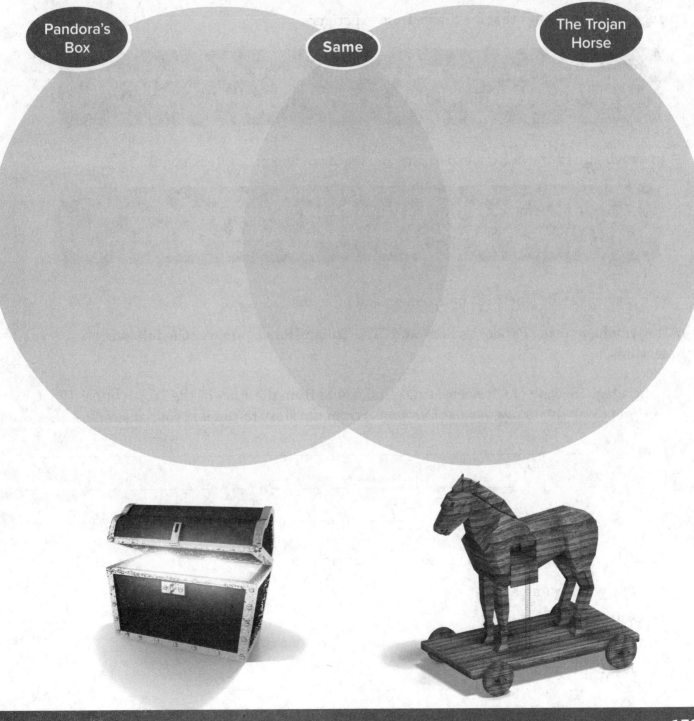

Pandora's Box

Same

The Trojan Horse

UNDERSTANDING IDIOMS, ADAGES, AND PROVERBS

Idioms are common expressions people use about certain situations or experiences.

> Example: **"We are all in the same boat,"** means that everyone is experiencing the same situation.

Adages are old sayings that are drawn from experience.

> Example: **"A stitch in time saves nine,"** means that if you fix a problem when it first starts, it will save you a great deal of trouble.

A **proverb** also is drawn from experience and teaches a lesson or offers advice.

> Example: **"The early bird catches the worm,"** means that a person who gets started right away on a task usually is the one to succeed.

Some sayings can be labeled as both adages and proverbs.

After you have read "Pandora's Box" and "The Trojan Horse," answer the following questions.

1. The adage "Beware of Greeks bearing gifts" comes from the story of the Trojan horse. What do you think this adage means? Use details from the story to support your answer.

   _____

   _____

   _____

2. Which proverb or adage can be used for "Pandora's Box"?

   A. She who hesitates is lost.

   B. Curiosity killed the cat.

   C. A watched pot never boils.

   D. It is better to be safe than sorry.

3. Look at the picture. "Don't cry over spilled milk." What do you think this idiom means?

_____

_____

_____

_____

4. Look at the following picture. What is happening in the picture? Write the idiom phrase.

_____

_____

_____

_____

Think about it. What does the phrase mean?

_____

_____

_____

5. Look at the following picture. What is happening in the picture? Write the idiom phrase.

_____

_____

_____

_____

Think about it. What does the phrase mean?

_____

_____

_____

CORRECTING SENTENCES

The word **fragment** means a piece of something. When we talk about sentence fragments, we are referring to pieces of or incomplete sentences. Notice the sentence fragments below.

> Example: **By hiding in the wooden horse. The Greek soldiers were able to sneak into the city of Troy.**
>
> Correction: By hiding in the wooden horse, the Greek soldiers were able to sneak into the city of Troy.

Fragments often look like sentences, but **they are missing either the subject or the predicate of the main clause (or thought) of the sentence.** The main clause is always made up of a subject and a predicate. **The subject is always a noun or pronoun,** and it usually is acting or being acted upon by the predicate. **The predicate is a verb or verb phrase that usually shows some form of action, although sometimes it describes the subject's state of being.** Without these two word parts, sentences do not make sense.

Run-on sentences are when two or more main clauses are being used in a sentence without being linked together with a simple (or coordinating) conjunction, separated by a colon or semicolon, or divided into two sentences by a period.

> Example: **Pandora opened the box Zeus was standing behind her.**
>
> Correction: When Pandora opened the box, Zeus was standing behind **her.**

In the paragraph below, circle fragments and underline the run-on sentences. Then using a separate piece of paper, revise the content of the paragraph using only complete and correctly punctuated sentences.

The story of Pandora's box is one of many Greek myths someone disobeys a warning and is sorry for it. For example. Icarus was a young man. Who given wings made of feathers and wax he could fly. His father Daedalus told him not to fly too close to the sun Icarus did not listen to his father. When he flew too close to the sun. The wax melted he fell out of the sky.

WRITE YOUR STORY

Have you ever given, or wanted to give, someone a special gift? Why did you want to give the gift? For whom did you buy or make the gift? Why was, or is, the gift special? How did the person react, or how do you imagine the person will react in the future, when receiving the gift?

Write a story about a time when you gave someone a gift, or write how you imagine it would be giving the perfect gift to someone special. Remember to add sensory details, or details from the five senses (sight, smell, touch, taste, and hearing) to make your story more interesting. Use dialogue and descriptive details, too. Use the graphic organizer to help you map out your story.

When? Where?	Who?	What is the reason?
_____	_____	_____
Sensory Detail?	Sensory Detail?	Why is the gift being given?
_____	_____	_____

Event 1

Sensory Detail?

Event 2

Sensory Detail?

Event 3

Sensory Detail?

Conclusion

REVIEW

Congratulations! You have completed the lessons in this section. Now you will have the chance to practice some of the skills you just learned.

Reading Fluency

Adults: Time your student reading aloud for one minute. Make a note of where your student is at the end of one minute. Subtract incorrect words from the total words read. (Your student should be able to read 110–140 words per minute.) Then, have your student continue reading to the end of the article and answer the questions that follow.

The Lion and the Mouse

One day, a lion woke up from a nap to see a tiny gray mouse tip-toeing past him. Upon   20
seeing the lion was awake, the mouse began to run as fast as he could—but it was too late!   40
Before he knew it, the mouse had been scooped up by one of the lion's giant paws and was   59
being dangled in front of the beast's large golden eyes.   69

    "What do I have here?" chuckled the lion. "A very tasty snack, I believe."   83

    "Please do not eat me!" pleaded the wriggling mouse. "Please let me go free!"   97

    "And why should I do that?"   103

    "Because someday you may need me to help you."   112

    "You help me? How can that be? You are so tiny! What could you ever do for me, the   131
King of the Jungle?" asked the lion, who started laughing so hard that he had tears in his   149
eyes. When the lion finished laughing, he put the mouse back on the ground.   163

    "Go free," the lion said, waving his paw for the mouse to leave.   176

    "Thank you, thank you!" squeaked this mouse. "I promise I will help you when you   191
need a friend."   194

    The lion grunted as the mouse scurried away.   202

    A few weeks later, the mouse heard the lion roaring. He followed the sound of the roars   219
and looked frantically for the lion. Then the mouse saw the King of the Jungle tied down   236
by several heavy ropes that were staked to the ground. He watched the lion struggle to free   253
himself, with no success.   257

    "What happened?" the mouse asked when he ran down to the lion.   269

    "A group of hunters captured me while I was sleeping. They went back to get more men   286
to take me their village." The lion sighed heavily. "I am doomed."   298

"Hold on," said the mouse. "Let me help." Before the lion could say another word,   313
the mouse began gnawing on one of the ropes. Soon the rope snapped into two pieces!   329
He jumped to the next piece of rope and began chewing that one as well. After several   346
minutes, the lion was freed from the ropes. The very grateful lion peered down at the   362
tiny mouse.   364

"I owe you an apology, my little friend. You were right. You have been a great help   381
to me. If you hadn't come along, I would still be in serious trouble."   395

"If you had eaten me," the mouse replied. "I would not be here to help you."   411

"You are so right," the lion smiled. "And I am glad to have you for a friend."   428

Words read in 1 minute – errors = WPM

Activity 1

Use "The Lion and the Mouse" to answer the following questions.

1. Match the proverb, adage, or idiom with the action of the lion and/or the mouse.

    1. the lion's response to the mouse's promise

    2. the mouse begging not to be eaten

    3. the lion being rescued by the mouse

    4. hunters having captured the lion

    a. a bird in the hand is worth two in the bush

    b. a friend in need is a friend indeed

    c. having a barrel of laughs

    d. throwing oneself on another's mercy

2. In the story, the lion is captured by hunters while he is sleeping. Can the adage, "What you don't know won't hurt you" be used for this part of the story? Why or why not? Use details from the story to explain your answer.

    _____

    _____

3. Which of the following two idioms best describes what the mouse did for the lion? Use details from the text to support your answer.

    A. "The mouse lent the lion a hand."

    B. "The mouse lent the lion an ear."

    _____

    _____

4. There is a Japanese proverb that says, "Eggs and promises are easily broken." Does this proverb describe the mouse's promise to the lion? Why or why not? Use details from the text to support your answer.

    _____

    _____

5. Can the proverb, "A difficult situation is when friendship is proven" be used about this story? Why or why not? Use details from the fable to support your answer.

    _____

    _____

Activity 2

Demonstrate the proper use of quotation marks and commas by completing the following activities.

1. Is this sentence punctuated correctly? If not, place the correct punctuation where needed.

   Although you are the King of the Jungle said the mouse, a small creature such as me can be helpful to you someday.

2. Place commas correctly into the following sentence.

   "When I saw you caught in the ropes" the mouse said "I had to help!"

3. Place quotation marks correctly into the following sentence

   I am so glad you kept your promise! said the lion. You are a true friend indeed.

4. Write two sentences of dialogue between the lion and the mouse, using commas and quotation marks correctly. Remember to add a period to the end of each sentence.

   _____

   _____

   _____

   _____

   _____

   _____

   _____

   _____

Let's apply the reading skills you covered in this section.

Use "The Lion and the Mouse" to answer the following questions.

1. Why was the lion in serious trouble? Use details from the story to support your answer.

   _____

   _____

2. How does the story describe the start of a friendship? Use details from the story to support your answer.

   _____

   _____

3. What is the **theme**, or moral, of the story?

   _____

   _____

4. Write a **summary** that tells what the story is about.

   _____

   _____

5. What is the **most** important event in the story? Use details from the text to support your answer.

   _____

   _____

6. Use details from the text to describe how the lion's feelings toward the mouse change in the story.

   _____

   _____

DISCOVER

Write Your Narrative

A narrative is a story that can be real or imagined. Many times, narratives are based on things that really happened to the writer.

In this section, you read a story about a mouse that helped a lion. What a great story to show that you are never too young or too small to make a difference in someone's life and lend a helping hand.

Have you ever helped someone who was in need? Was this person a family member, friend, or neighbor? What was the problem, and how did you help? How did it make you feel? Did the person help you at a later time?

Write a story about an experience you may have had, or you can make up a story in which you helped someone or someone helped you. Use the graphic organizer to write a strong introduction and descriptive details that support your ideas. Write a series of events that leads up to the most important event. Use dialogue and description to develop your story and/or show the responses of characters in the situations. Use transitional words and phrases such as "because" and "then." Remember to use concrete words and phrases, and sensory details (touch, taste, smell, seeing, and hearing) to describe the experience. Finally, write a conclusion that sums up how you felt about the experience.

Who is in your story?

Where and when does your story take place?

What is the most important event in the story?

Introduction (Who is in the story? What is happening? Where and when does the story take place?):

Event 1 (What happens first?):

Event 2 (What happens next?):

Event 3 (What is the most important event?):

Conclusion (How do you feel about the experience?):

Transitional Words and Phrases:

in fact	such as	because	for example	including	first
however	certainly	in general	like	to be sure	second
surely	namely	truly	indeed	as well as	third
especially	surprisingly	therefore	in contrast	although	at the same time
moreover	likewise	additionally	because	again	after all
usually	suddenly	next	since	until	meanwhile

Answer Key

Reading Foundational Skills

Unit 1–Fluency: Read with Purpose and Understanding

Lesson 1–Getting a New Pet

Page 5. Guided Questions: 1. The author says you should look for holes in the yard and fence. A swimming pool may be dangerous. You should also look indoors for loose wires; 2. Answers may vary. Sample response: Two responsibilities are feeding your new pet and making sure it has fresh water; 3. Answers may vary. Sample response: I think new pets need love and affection because it makes them feel good and like a part of the family; 4. Places to call home are important because it gives the new pet a place of its own and makes it feel wanted.

Lesson 2–Atlas, the Incredible Robot

Page 7. Guided Questions: 1. Robots are needed to help in disaster situations so that human beings are not put at great risk; 2. Front-runners refer to those who are ahead of the others in a competition; 3. Atlas is like a human because it has joints, arms, and can follow directions; 4. Atlas robots are different from humans because the robots have super strength and are able to move heavy objects that humans cannot move by themselves.

Lesson 3–The Art of the Postal Stamp

Page 9. Guided Questions: 1. A stamp's design is determined by the Postal Service Art Director; 2. Especially means mainly. The Bugs Bunny stamp needed to appeal to mainly children; 3. Some collectors worried that Bugs Bunny was too commercial and that it would take away from stamps based on important historical figures; 4. Answers will vary. Sample response: Warner Bros. created many sketches, but the Postal Service picked the theme of the mailbox for all the Looney Tunes stamps.

Lesson 4–Bare Bones: A Study Group

Page 11. Guided Questions: 1. They are studying for an upcoming quiz on the parts of a bone; 2. Periosteum is a thin layer on the outer surface of the bone that contains nerves and blood vessels. The pronunciation guide helps to say the word clearly, while words like outer surface helps

to define the word; 3. The compact bone and the cancellous helps to protect the bone marrow; 4. She compares bone marrow to jelly. Explanations will vary. Sample response: This means that it is soft and gushy.

Reading and Writing: Informational Texts

Unit 2–Famous Scientists

Lesson 1–Dedicated to a Cure

Page 17. Finding Main Ideas and Details: 1. D; 2. B; 3. Answers may vary. Sample: She truly cared about other people and wanted to save people's lives; 4. A

Page 18. Getting More Information with Visual Aids: 1. After; 2. Before; 3. Two years; 4. 44 years old; 5. B

Page 19. Understanding the Clues: 1. B; 2. B; 3. C

Page 20. Using Relative Pronouns: 1. Who; 2. Whose; 3. Which; 4. Where

Page 21. Learning Progressive Verb Tense: 1. The group of scientists will arrive by 7:00 p.m.; 2. My brother was finishing his chemistry homework; 3. The students will study for their physics test; 4. Researchers are searching for a cure for cancer.

Challenge: Answers will vary. Sample: Alexander Graham Bell was a scientist who is known for inventing the telephone. Before he invented the telephone, he was a speech teacher just like his father and grandfather. He worked at a school for the deaf. His concern for the deaf, whom he taught, led him to experiment with different devices that could help them to communicate. In 1874, he found a partner, Thomas Watson, who worked along with him to help bring his vision to life. After many experiments, they successfully made the first "phone call" in 1876. Many people found this new way of communication quite amazing. Mr. Bell's invention has helped many people and has changed the world. By inventing the telephone, Mr. Bell made it possible for us to speak with our friends and family, and hear their voice, even if they live in another country very far away.

Lesson 2—An Unusual Mind

Page 23. Mapping the Main Idea and Supporting Details: Main Idea: Einstein's theories changed the world of science and made him one of the most famous scientists in history; Detail 1: During his "miracle" year, Einstein wrote four papers that changed physics and the way scientists thought about time and space; Detail 2: This theory changed what scientists believed about gravity; Detail 3: A few years later, in 1921, Einstein was awarded the Nobel Prize in Physics because his discovery was very important to many areas of science; Summary: Albert Einstein was one of the most famous scientists in history because his theories changed what scientists believed about gravity. He was awarded the Nobel Prize in Physics because his discovery was very important to many areas of science.

Page 24. Understanding Cause and Effect: Cause: He did not learn to speak as early as most children his age; Cause: At the age of five, his father gave him a compass; Effect: He thought in pictures rather than words; Effect: Einstein changed physics and the way scientists thought about time and space; Cause: His Theory of Relativity was very important to many areas of science.

Page 25. Understanding the Clues: 1. D; 2. A; 3. B; 4. Revolutionize: To change something very much or completely. Possible context clues: New, concepts, change

Page 26. Helping Verbs: Activity 1: Answers will vary. Samples: 1. If Jackie were a scientist, she might be able to invent a cure for the common cold; 2. Jeffraisha said she might go to the science fair this weekend; 3. Lance says he may also attend the science fair this weekend; 4. May I help you with the science project? Activity 2: 1. must; 2. could; 3. will

Unit 3—Famous Artists and Composers

Lesson 1—Ludwig van Beethoven—A Heart for Music

Page 30. Finding Main Ideas and Details, Summarizing: 1. B; 2. C; 3. "In 1783, Neefe was so impressed with Beethoven that he said of him in the *Magazine of Music,* "If he continues like this, he will be, without a doubt, the new Mozart." 4. Answers will vary. Sample: Beethoven did not let his loss of hearing stop him from continuing to create the best music in history. I should not let any disability or challenge that I may be facing prevent me from doing great things with my life.

Page 31. Relationships Between Events: 1. Answers will vary. Example: He played his first concert at age 5, and before age 12, he published his first composition; Neefe was

quoted in *Magazine of Music* saying that he would become the next Mozart; 2. B; 3. Answers may vary. Example: When he learned that he was going deaf, he became so sad that he wanted to focus his remaining time that he could hear on creating more music. In 1802, he wrote a famous text about his feelings. Then he took his pain and turned it into some of the most beautiful music that ever composed; 4. It was so original the musicians were unable to play it after weeks of practicing. Beethoven played the piano with strong emotion, in a way that showed how he felt about his life and being alive. This kind of symphony had never been played before. It changed people's understanding of what a symphony could be. 5. Student should circle choices A, D, and E.

Page 32. Vocabulary Development and Use: 1. D; 2. C; 3. A symphony is a musical piece. Clues: "*Eroica Symphony,* was one of his most outstanding and original works," "In this symphony, Beethoven played the piano using broad strokes of sound to tell his audience how he felt about life and being alive," "This masterpiece was so great and different from anything anyone had ever heard that the musicians could not learn how to play it, despite weeks of practice." 4. D

Page 33. Prepositional Phrases: Activity 1: under the piano (prep. phrase) under (preposition) piano (direct object); during the concert (prep. phrase) during (preposition) concert (direct object); 2. After our big concert (prep. phrase) After (preposition) concert (direct object); with them (prep. phrase) with (preposition) them (direct object); 3. In Vienna, Austria (prep. phrase) In (preposition) Vienna, Austria (direct object); for most of his life (prep. phrase) for (preposition) life (direct object); 4. By the time (prep. phrase) by (preposition) time (direct object); in public places (prep. phrase) in (preposition) places (direct object); Activity 2: Answers will vary. Examples: 1. The concert is right around the corner; 2. The teacher's violin is outside the auditorium; 3. Toward the end of the night, Jessie played his violin; 4. My grandfather became a professional piano player without taking lessons.

Page 34. Clarifying Commonly Confused Words: 1. write; 2. too, to; 3. allowed, break; 4. our, their; 5. they're

Page 35. Choosing Punctuation for Effect: Activity 1: 1. I remembered the entire musical poem (it was not easy) and recited it for my class; 2. Did you get your permission slip (the pink one) for the music museum trip tomorrow? 3. Be sure to read both music articles (7 pages each) before you take the test; 4. Some kids do not like music history—but all my life I have loved the piano. 5. We have to compose our own songs (simple ones) for our music class project.

Activity 2: 1. Yes, my mother will come on our class trip tomorrow; 2. There is so much to learn about the Renaissance period—I can't wait to go on the trip tomorrow; 3. Good! I was hoping that we would go on a field trip this month; 4. Uh-Oh! Sharon forgot to bring in her signed permission slip; 5. The museum trip will be a lot of fun—in fact we will be taking two tours.

Activity 3: My sister Syntisha's music class went on a field trip. They went to the New Music Museum. Thankfully, they had a wonderful tour guide, Mr. Deepak. Syntisha said it was the best tour she ever had—the worst one was last year at the planetarium. Her class decided to take the 1950s Music Tour (she loves Elvis) and the Music History Tour—it had a brand new section for young artists. The teacher gave a challenge to the class. She said, "Whoever takes the best notes (complete notes) and emails them to me tonight—wins a free homework pass." Wow, what a cool teacher Syntisha has! My sister took a lot of notes. When she got home, she sent an email to her teacher. *"Mrs. Chin, thank you for taking us to the museum today. Here are the notes I took (see attachment) I hope you like them. Wow! I learned a lot of great things today. It was fun! See you in class tomorrow. Sincerely, Syntisha."*

Stop and Think! Units 1–3 Review

Page 39. Activity 1: 1. Whose; 2. Who; Activity 2: 1. Going to create; 2. Was drawing; Activity 3: 1. Should; 2. Shall; Activity 4: Answers will vary: 1. Every Sunday, after we eat breakfast, my father reads me the comics; 2. The boy is looking around the house for the comics; 3. I am deciding which comic I like the most. It is between Garfield and Peanuts. Activity 5: Answers will vary using too, two, and to: 1. Sample response: My two favorite cartoonists are Charles Schulz and Dr. Seuss. 2. Is your teacher having your class write cartoon strips too? 3. I am going to watch the Charlie Brown special on television tonight; Activity 6: 1. Whoopee! 2. (found below) Activity 7: 1. A cartoonist is a person who creates a drawing that tells a brief, funny story. 2. The word silliness is a context clue for humor.

Stop and Think! Units 3–4 Understand

Page 42. Activity 1: 1. Dr. Seuss is one of the most famous children's book authors in the world; 2. Once Dr. Seuss's first book hit the market, it changed the world of children's literature. *The Cat in The Hat* became one of the best-selling series, Beginner Books, to teach children how to read. Dr. Suess's books have sold over half a billion copies; 3. C; 4. She told him rhymes when he was a child.

Page 43. Activity 2: 1. He won the Caldecott and New York Library Lion awards for *McElligot's Pool*. He won the Caldecott and Laura Ingalls Wilder awards for *If I Ran the Zoo*. 2. 1949

Unit 4—On the Route to Discovery and Innovation

Lesson 1—Diamond Rain

Page 47. Finding Main Ideas and Details: 1. A; 2. B; 3. D

Page 48. Explaining Steps in a Process: 1. D; 2. B; 3. Afterward the graphite falls for around 4,000 miles, increasing the pressure until it turns into a diamond. Understanding Text Structure: 1. D; 2. D

Page 49. Vocabulary Development and Use 1. A; 2. A; 3. D

Page 50. Using Commas in Compound Sentences: Activity 1: 1. Alexandria loved the diamond ring, so she bought it; 2. Wyatt wrote a report on diamond rain, and he included information that he learned in science class; 3. Jupiter is producing diamonds, but scientists cannot reach them; 4. Correct; 5. You can choose to study Jupiter, or you can choose to study Saturn. Activity 2: Answers will vary. Samples: 1. Diamonds are popular gemstones, but they are expensive; 2. Saturn is a planet made almost entirely of gas, and so is Jupiter; 3. Marjory wanted to work at NASA, yet she did not apply for the job; 4. Scientists are sending a spacecraft to study Jupiter's gravity, and they are sending one to Saturn.

Lesson 2—Solar Roadways

Page 52. Finding Main Ideas and Details: 1. Solar roadways are a new paving system that would improve and change the world as we know it; 2. Answers will vary. Sample: 1. LED lights would be painted on the road to reduce vehicle accidents by seventy percent. The lights would allow drivers to see better at night and provide a warning when deer or other wild animals were entering the road; 2. Therefore, business and homeowners would receive electricity for telephones, cable TV, and even the Internet from the power grid that runs off of the sun's energy; 3. Electric roads would make electric vehicles (EV) that run on batteries more user friendly. EV owners could recharge their batteries in parking lots or rest stops; 3. Answers will vary. Sample: Solar roadways would change the world as we know it. Solar roadways use glass panels to collect energy from the sun that would melt snow, eliminate power outages, and cut greenhouse gas pollution by nearly seventy-five percent.

Page 53. Describing Scientific Concepts: Feature: Heating element; Effect: Prevent snow and ice buildup; Feature: LED lights; Effect: prevent accidents by lighting up the road; Feature: Solar panels; create clean drinking water in developing nations; Feature: Power grid; Effect: Carry electricity to business and homeowners; Feature: Solar panels; Effect: produce clean energy from the sun.

Answer Key

Page 54. Understanding Text Structure: 1. A; 2. D

Page 55. Vocabulary Development and Use: 1. A; 2. B; 3. Clue for user-friendly: EV owners could recharge their batteries in parking lots or rest stops. It will be easy to keep a car running with solar roadways; Clue for developing nation: Solar panels can provide needed power to create clean drinking water in developing nations. If a country does not have clean water, it must be underdeveloped.

Page 56. Using Synonyms: Power—Energy, Panel—Board, Prevent—Stop, Grid—Network, Decrease—Lessen, Environment—Surroundings, Benefit—Advantage

Page 57. Correcting Sentences: Activity 1: 1. Correct; 2. LED lights on highways; 3. Heating elements on the surface of roadways; 4. Correct; Activity 2: 1. This sentence should be underlined; 2. This sentence should not be underlined; Activity 3: Answers will vary. Sample answer. 1. Solar roadways are all over the city; 2. Solar roadways can be placed on driveways; 3. If we had a power outage, the lights would go out; 4. The lights went out, so we hid under the bed; 5. The solar panels melted the snow, so we didn't shovel the driveway.

Unit 5—Appreciate our Land

Lesson 1—Hiking the Appalachian Trail

Page 63. Finding Main Ideas and Details: 1. A; 2. Answers will vary. Sample response: The Appalachian Trail is a long hiking trail that goes from Georgia to Maine. People who want to hike on the Appalachian Trail should plan their trip carefully and pack the right equipment. They should also be respectful of nature while they are hiking on the trail. Hiking the Appalachian Trail can be a fun experience for people who follow these tips; Explaining Details: 1. Answers will vary. Sample response: The Appalachian Trail is home to many plants and animals, and leaving trash or picking plants would be disrespectful; 2. C

Page 64. Understanding Text Structure: 1. C; 2. D; 3. B; 4. D

Page 65. Explaining Reasons and Evidence: Answers will vary. Sample evidences: Hikers need water because hiking is strenuous exercise; Hikers need food so they do not run out of energy; Hikers need sturdy shoes because hiking is mainly walking and climbing; Hikers need comfortable clothing because they will be moving around; Hikers need a jacket because the weather might change during their trip

Page 66. Understanding Root Words: 1. A; 2. C; 3. D; 4. B

Page 67. Using Antonyms: 1. B; 2. D; 3. C; 4. A

Lesson 2—The Grand Canyon

Page 70. Finding Main Ideas and Details: 1. C; 2. B; 3.

Answers will vary. Sample response: The Grand Canyon is a place that many people visit because it is beautiful and unique. It was formed by erosion from the Colorado River and is millions of years old. It is also home to lots of plants and animals, including some that only live in the Grand Canyon. The Grand Canyon was made into a national park to protect it, but people can still visit it and do lots of things there as long as they try to leave no trace.

Page 71. Explaining Relationships: Answers will vary. Sample responses: see views of the canyon from lookout points; learn about the canyon at education centers and museums; go hiking and camping around and inside the canyon; take a mule ride into the canyon; raft down the Colorado River inside the canyon; 2. Answers may vary. Sample response: It took millions of years for the Grand Canyon to form. The Colorado River eroded many layers of rock and dust year after year. As more and more rock was carried away by the river, the canyon was formed.

Page 72. Understanding Text Structure: 1. A; 2. D; Identifying Reasons and Evidence: Answers will vary. Sample evidences: The Grand Canyon is unique because rock layers are visible there that are not visible in other places and scientists need to be able to study them; The Grand Canyon is home to at least 20 species of animals that do not live anywhere else in the world, and for those species to survive, the canyon must be protected; Protecting the Grand Canyon ensures that other people in the future will be able to enjoy it the same way many others already have.

Page 73. Explaining Data: 1. 277 miles; 2. C; 3. B; 4. Yes; in at least one place, the canyon is only 600 feet wide, but the average depth of the canyon is 1 mile, or 5,280 feet, which is a greater distance than 600 feet.

Page 74. Using Reference Materials: 1. Noun; 2. Student should underline Definition B.

Page 75. Synonyms: 1. A; 2. D

Unit 6—In The Wild

Lesson 1—The Bald Eagle: An Endangered Species Success Story

Page 79. Finding Main Ideas and Details: 1. A; 2. C; Explaining Ideas and Events: 1. B; 2. A

Page 80. Understanding Text Structure: 1. Answers will vary. Sample: The overall structure is chronological, although each paragraph does present a problem/solution setup as well. If the paragraphs were switched, the sentence, "Still the bald eagle was in trouble," would not make sense because the original paragraph 3 sets up that statement by talking about how the U.S. government sought to protect the bald eagle;

2. Answers will vary. Sample: Paragraph 2 provides information about the bald eagle's habitat and how many eggs are laid each year. Paragraph 3 talks about how these habitats were destroyed. Paragraph 4 talks about how DDT caused the bald eagle's eggs to break easily; therefore, the number of eaglets being born decreased. Both paragraphs 3 and 4 map back to paragraph 2; 3. Answers will vary. Sample: If paragraph 5 were placed after paragraph 1, the content would be confusing because the rest of the article would be about how the bald eagle almost became extinct.

Page 81. Using Charts to Gather Information: Answers will vary. Sample: The bald eagle population dramatically increased over 43 years. Yes, the chart supports the information in the article, but it also provides more details than the article does about the number of bald eagle nesting pairs over the years.

Page 82. Mastering Capitalization: 1. The United States government passed several laws to protect the bald eagle; 2. The U.S. Environmental Protection Agency stopped the use of DDT; 3. The Endangered Species Act created a list of animals that were close to extinction; 4. The Migratory Bird Treaty Act protected bald eagles when they migrated, or flew to, Mexico and other countries; Challenge: Misspelled Word: revulution, declaired, gloreus, populore, freedom, independence; Correct Spelling: revolution, declared, glorious, popular, freedom, independence; Meaning: revolution—an attempt by a group of people to begin a new government by ending the old one, declared—announced, glorious—very wonderful or delightful, popular—liked by a large number of people, freedom—the state of being free, independence—free from support or control; Words that need to be capitalized: Americans, British, Even

Lesson 2—The Plan for the Bald Eagle

Page 85. Compare and Contrast Articles: Answers may vary, but students should list how the eagle almost became extinct 50 years ago, the number of bald eagle nesting pairs 50 years ago, the number of nesting pairs in 2007, and the government legislation to protect the bird; 2. Answers may vary, but students may write about how in the first article, there is a discussion of the bald eagle as a national symbol, now it lives in the wild, and how DDT nearly made the bird extinct; For the second article, students may list details about the Post-delisting Monitoring Plan.

Page 86. Combining Information from Two Texts: Answers may vary, but students should write a paragraph with a topic idea about the bald eagle and provide supporting details from both articles.

Lesson 3—Fishzilla: The Snakehead Fish

Page 90. Finding Main Ideas and Details: 1. C; 2. B

Page 91. Explaining Ideas and Events: 1. c; 2. d; 3. a; 4. b; 2: A; Explaining Reasons and Evidence: 1. Answers will vary, but students should address the phrase and find evidence from the text to support their statements. 2. Answers will vary, but students should address the phrase and find evidence from the text to support their statements.

Page 92. Understanding the Clues: 1. D; 2. C

Page 93. Vocabulary Development and Use: 1. Answers will vary, but students should discuss how snakeheads are freshwater fish and live in water, and how fish also can live in an aquarium; 2. Living in water; 3. Answers will vary. Sample: The government claims that the chemicals in the water will not harm people or aquatic life. 4. A group of people, animals, or parts of things that function together; 5. A group of animals that function in the same environment; 6. Answers will vary. Sample: Scientists believe pesticides are harming the ecosystem.

Page 94. Using Reference Materials: 1. A; 2. Adjective; 3. Three syllables; 4. An animal that eats other animals; Choosing the Right Words: Wriggling means squirming along the ground. Answers will vary, but students might suggest that the word "moving" does not create as visual of an image as "wriggling" does.

Stop and Think! Units 4–6 Review

Page 96. Activity 1: 1. b; 2. d; 3. a; 4. c; 2. The word endangered means that the species is close to extinction, where threatened means that the species is close to being endangered; 3. Answers will vary, but discuss a particular habitat for a wild creature; 4. It means the animal is no longer protected by the ESA; 5. No, the grizzly is native to the American West.

Page 97. Activity 2: Samples: 1. Bald eagle—a large eagle of the United States and Canada that is dark brown with a white head and tail; Grizzly bear—a large, fierce bear found in northwestern parts of North America, with a coat that varies from grayish to brown; Snakehead fish—an invasive fish native to Asia; 2. Match: 1. d; 2. e; 3. c; 4. a; 5. b

Stop and Think! Units 4–6 Understand

Page 98. 1. The grizzly bear will remain a threatened species under the ESA until an agreement can be made whether or not to delist this animal; 2. Sample: However, nature groups fought to keep the bear protected, so the grizzly bear was again listed as threatened in 2009; 3. A process in which an endangered or threatened animal is protected from harm; 4.

To rest or remain inactive; 5. That the bear is very powerful and has been part of the American West for a long time. Details such as, "In the early 1800s, over 50,000 grizzly bears roamed across the parts of the West," and "A huge hump on their back that is all muscle," and so on, should be used; 6. More than 600 grizzly bears are alive in Yellowstone now.

Reading and Writing: Literature

Unit 7—Short Fiction

Lesson 1—Rikki-Tikki-Tavi

Page 107. Finding Main Ideas and Details: 1. D; 2. A long time ago, in India. Other possible answers: In a family's home and garden; 3. B; 4. C; 5. 3, 2, 5, 1, 4; 6. Rikki-Tikki-Tavi is a small furry animal with a bushy tail. He is not very old. He is curious because he likes to explore the house and garden. He is also very brave, because he fights the snakes. Usually he is not mean, but when he is angry, his eyes get red and he turns into a killer.

Page 109. Understanding Text Structure: The following words should have checkmarks: Sentences, Paragraphs, Dialogue (Conversation). The following words should NOT have checkmarks: Stanzas, Rhyming words, Meter; 2. a. The student should have circled "No, the story is not a poem"; b: Answers will vary. Sample: Poetry uses stanzas, meter, and rhyming words. The story does not have any of these, so it is not written in poetry.

Page 110. Prose or Poetry: Answers will vary. Sample: I can tell the characters are talking because there are quote marks around what they say. There are also words like, "he said," that let me know someone is talking.

Page 111. Understanding Point of View: 1. D; 2. Third person. Answers will vary. Sample: I know that the story is written from third-person point of view because the narrator does not use words like "I" and "we." When the narrator talks about Rikki-Tikki-Tavi and the other characters, he uses words like "he," "she," "it," and "they." An example is "he explored the house," talking about Rikki-Tikki.

Page 112. Connecting Literature and Art: 1. C; 2. Answers will vary. Sample: I would draw Nag and Rikki-Tikki still fighting but with Teddy's father standing in the corner, pointing his gun at Nag to kill him; 3. B; 4. While there is not a correct answer, Nagaina is the best answer. Answers will vary based on the student's answer to Question #3. Two samples: [A student who did not initially choose Nagaina:] Yes, Nagaina. Before, I thought that it was Nag running

from Rikki-Tikki-Tavi, but Nag dies in the part of the story that we read. The small brown snake dies too. At the end of the part we read, Rikki-Tikki is planning to hunt for Nagaina and her eggs. The snake in the picture has an egg in its mouth and is still alive so far, so it must be Nagaina; [A student who initially chose Nagaina:] No, [blank]. Before, I thought it was probably Nagaina because she runs away from Rikki-Tikki after he bites her in the part of the story that we read. Also, the snake has an egg in its mouth and Nagaina talks about her eggs. Now I am sure it is Nagaina because the other snakes are already dead before the second part of the story.

Page 114. Understanding Similes: 1. B; 2. There are two possible answers: "tail that fluffs up like a bottle-brush" and "swayed back and forth like a dandelion tuft in the wind"; 3. Answers will vary. Sample: In the dirt nearby, there was a snake, small and brown like a leather shoelace. 4. Answers will vary. Sample: Nagaina was as quiet as a mouse when she snuck up behind Rikki-Tikki; Nagaina was angry like a swarm of bees after Rikki-Tikki bit her on the back.

Lesson 2—The Lady, Or the Tiger?

Page 117. Determining Themes, Characters, and Conclusions: 1. B; 2. The princess; 3. D; 4. C; 5. A; 6. The princess wants to find out which room will have the lady and which one will have the tiger. She finds this information by talking to people and paying them for it; 7. Answers will vary. Sample: The princess must be smart, because she figures out how to get the information. However, she is not always honest, because she is willing to pay people for it, even though no one is supposed to be able to find out.

Page 119. Understanding Metaphors: 1. B; 2. First blank: Young man; Second blank: Marble statue; Explanation: Answers will vary. Sample: The metaphor tells me that the young man is standing very still in the center of the arena, not even moving, like a statue. He is also like a statue because people are looking at him, but he is not responding; 3. First blank: Tiger; Second blank: Lady; 4. D

Unit 8—Poetry

Lesson 1—An Emerald is as Green as Grass

Page 126. Drawing Conclusions and Understanding Details: 1. B; 2. D; 3. D; 4. Answers will vary. Samples: "A flint lies in the mud," "A diamond is a brilliant stone," "A diamond catches the world's desire." 5. B, C

Page 127. Finding Context Clues: 1. B, D; 2. B, C

Page 129. Learn the Structure of Poems and Prose: 1. Desire and fire; 2. Answers will vary. Samples: "Green as grass," "ruby red," "flint holds fire"; 3. C; 4. Yes; additional answers will vary. Correct answers should note that putting the emphasis on certain syllables is part of the meter. Additionally, answers should note that the number of syllables alternates from line to line.

Page 130. Understanding Similes: 1. D; 2. Answers may be in any order: "red as blood," "blue as heaven"; 3. Answers will vary but should be one of the following: an emerald is green, a ruby is red, a sapphire is blue (alternatively, a sapphire shines blue, a sapphire is blue and shiny, etc.); 4. Answers will vary depending on which simile the student chose to rewrite in Question 3. A sample answer follows using "A ruby red as blood" and "A ruby is red." How are they the same? Both sentences tell you that a ruby is red; How are they different? The sentence that I wrote is not a simile. It just says the ruby is red. The simile compares the red color of the ruby to the red color of blood; Which one gives a better description? The simile, "A ruby red as blood." Why? Because it compares the red of the ruby to something that most people know, the color of red blood. Even if someone had never seen a ruby before, they would be able to know what kind of red it is because they know what blood looks like.

Lesson 2—Fog

Page 133. Drawing Conclusions and Understanding Details: 1. B; 2. D; 3. C; 4. Adjective: Little / Word Describing: Feet (or cat feet); Adjective: Silent / Word Describing: Haunches [Very unlikely answer] Adjective: Cat / Word Describing: Feet

Challenge: Answers will vary. Sample: The word little in front of cat feet makes it sound like the fog is tiptoeing quietly. The word silent also makes the fog sound quiet. The detail from the describing words lets me know that the fog is quiet like the cat.

Page 134. Understanding Metaphors: 1. B; 2. A; 3. Answers will vary. Samples: The fog comes into the city as quietly as a cat, stays for a little while, and then leaves. The fog moves through the city like a cat; 4. Answers will vary and will likely be based on student's answer to question 3, above. Samples: The fog comes into the city quietly, stays for a little while, and then leaves. The fog moves through the city; 5. Answers will vary. Samples: Do all of the sentences give you the same basic information about fog? Why or why not? Yes, because all the sentences tell you that the fog moves through the city. OR No, because all of the sentences talk about the fog but only two of them talk about how the fog is like a cat; 6. Student will most likely choose "metaphor poem" or "simile sentence"; 7. Student will most likely choose "metaphor poem" or "simile sentence." Why? The metaphor poem would be the easiest to explain to someone because most people know what a cat is like so it would be easy to explain what the fog is like to them.

Stop and Think Units! 7–8 Review

Page 139. Activity 1: Answers will vary widely. Any answer that seems to reflect use of context clues should be accepted. 2. Sample definitions follow a dictionary. a. Near; b. Amusement or laughter; c. Rising, springing, or gushing, as water; d. Light in movement, graceful, delicate; Activity 2: 1. C; 2. There are two possible answers: "World" and "Fairy star"; 3. D; 4. Light, feather; moonshine rays (feather and moonshine rays can be in no particular order); 5. Two possible answers: A feather is as light as a moonshine ray. A moonshine ray is as light as a feather.

Stop and Think! Units 7–8 Understand

Page 141. 1. Answers will vary stylistically but should include something about the bubble popping; 2. B; 3. A. 2; B. 4; C. 3; D. 1; 4. Answers will vary but should recognize that the majority of the poem contains positive emotions and mood. Sample: Most of the poem is happy. The writer of the poem thinks that the bubbles are beautiful and describes them as playing and full of mirth, which means laughter. The writer thinks of bubbles as little worlds where fairies live, which makes the poem feel imaginative; 5. Answers will vary. Students will most likely indicate that the mood changes in the last stanza but not necessarily. Samples: [A student who believes the mood changes]: Yes, the mood changes at the end when the writer describes the bubble popping. The writer says that the droplets formed when the bubble pops are like tears, which makes the reader think of crying as sad things. The mood becomes sad when the bubble pops. [A student who does not believe the mood changes]: No, the mood stays the same through the entire poem. Even though the bubble pops in the last stanza, the writer does not make it sound like a sad thing, because he uses an exclamation point. It is surprising when the bubble pops, but the poem stays happy.

Unit 9—Mythology and Fables

Lesson 1—Pandora's Box

Page 147. Determining Themes: 1. D; 2. B; Describing Characters, Settings, and Events: 1. A; 2. C

Page 148. Determining the Meaning of Phrases: 1. Answers will vary, but students may say that the phrase means a person is in a situation where his or her decision could create a great deal of trouble for others. Details from the text include Pandora making a poor decision based on a desire and the world suffers from it; 2. Answers will vary, but students may say that the sentence means that no matter how bad a situation may become, people can hope it will get better.

Page 149. Using Commas and Quotation Marks: 1. "Because my curiosity was so strong," said Pandora, "I had to open the box." 2. "If you had followed the note," Zeus responded, "then the world would still be free of hardships." 3. "I am very sorry," Pandora cried; 4."You are forgiven," Zeus smiled.

Lesson 2—The Trojan Horse

Page 151. Determining Themes: 1. B; 2. C; Using Details and Examples: 1. A; 2. D

Page 152. Comparing and Contrasting Point of View: 1. Answers may vary, but students may say that both Pandora and the Trojan soldiers are curious about a gift; 2. Answers may vary, but students may say that Pandora was sorry for creating trouble for others where the Trojan soldiers were sorry for creating trouble for themselves; 3. A. Story title: Pandora's Box; Example from story: Answers will vary, but sentence example should use first person; B. Story title: The Trojan Horse; Example from story: Answers will vary, but sentence example should use third person.

Page 153. Comparing and Contrasting Themes: 1. Answers may vary, but students may mention that both stories involve a mysterious gift that, when opened, creates trouble for Pandora and the Trojans, respectively. While Pandora feels guilty for the consequences created by her actions, the Trojans are upset because they lost the war after being tricked.

Page 154. Understanding Idioms, Adages, and Proverbs: 1. The Greeks were the enemy, so the meaning of the adage is do not trust gifts from an enemy, as it may be a trick; 2. B; 3. Do not be upset about making a mistake, since you cannot change that now; 4. The picture shows dogs and cats falling from the sky and a boy holding an umbrella. Idiom phrase: It's raining cats and dogs. The phrase means it is raining really hard; 5. A girl is reaching her hand up toward the stars. Idiom phrase: Reaching for the stars. The phrase means do the best that you can do to make your dreams come true.

Page 156. Correcting Sentences: The story of Pandora's box is one of many Greek myths someone disobeys a warning and is sorry for it. Circle: For example. Icarus was a young man. Who given wings made of feathers and wax he could fly. His father Daedalus told him not to fly too close to the sun Icarus did not listen to his father. Circle: When he flew

too close to the sun. The wax melted he fell out of the sky. Paragraph revision: The story of Pandora's box is one of many Greek myths where someone disobeys a warning and is sorry for it. For example, Icarus was a young man who was given wings made of feathers and wax so he could fly. His father, Daedalus, told him not to fly too close to the sun. Icarus did not listen to his father. When he flew too close to the sun, the wax melted, and he fell out of the sky.

Stop and Think! Unit 9 Review

Page 160. Activity 1: 1. c; 2. d; 3. b; 4. a; 2. No, because if the lion knew he was being hunted, he would not have fallen asleep; 3. "The mouse lent the lion a hand." Students should discuss how the mouse helps out by gnawing the ropes; 4. No, because the mouse keeps his promise; 5. Yes, because the mouse proves he is a friend when the lion is in trouble. Activity 2: "Although you are the King of the Jungle," said the mouse, "a small creature such as me can be helpful to you someday." 2 "When I saw you caught in the ropes," the mouse said, "I had to help!" 3. "I am so glad you kept your promise!" said the lion. "You are a true friend indeed." 4. When the hunters returned to where they had tied up the lion, one of them said, "Those ropes were so tight! How did he get out of them?" 5. Answers will vary. Sample: "Mouse, you are my very best friend," the lion said, "I will do anything for you!" "You are my very best friend too, Lion!" exclaimed mouse.

Stop and Think! Unit 9 Understand

Page 162. 1. The lion was going to be taken back to the village by the hunters. Most likely he would be killed or put on display. "The King of the Jungle tied down by several heavy ropes that were staked to the ground," and "He watched the lion struggle to free himself, but with no success," "The lion sighed heavily. 'I am doomed.'" 2. Friendships can be made when each person or thing helps the other. Phrases such as "Because someday you may need me to help you," "And I am glad to have you for a friend"; 3. Never underestimate what someone can do; 4. A lion captures a mouse and then sets it free, only to be saved by it when he is captured himself; 5. When the lion is being set free from the ropes. Students can use details such as, "Soon the rope snapped into two pieces!" "After several minutes, the lion was free from the ropes"; 6. The lion laughs at the mouse at first and then he apologizes to him because the mouse is right. Phrases such as, "You help me? How can that be? You are so tiny!" and "I owe you an apology, my little friend. You were right."